Alamo Legacy

Always Cross The line!

Alamo Legacy

Alamo Descendants
Remember the Alamo

Ron Jackson

EAKIN PRESS ★ Austin, Texas

FIRST EDITION

Copyright © 1997
By Ron Jackson

Published in the United States of America
By Eakin Press
An Imprint of Sunbelt Media, Inc.
P.O. Drawer 90159 ★ Austin, TX 78709-0159

ISBN 1-57168-097-7

Library of Congress Cataloging-in-Publication Data

Jackson, Ron, 1966–
    Alamo legacy : Alamo descendants remember the Alamo / by Ron Jackson.
      p.   cm.
    Includes index.
    ISBN 1-57168-097-7
    1. Alamo (San Antonio, Tex.) — Siege, 1836. 2. Alamo (San Antonio, Tex.) — Siege, 1836 — Sources.
F390.J136   1996
976.4'03–dc20   96-15457
                                        CIP

To Jeannia, Joseph, and Ashley.

"Some things are worth dying for."

Contents

vi

Foreword

Long ago, I fell under the spell of the Alamo. The story of the defense of that mission-turned-fortress has been a special part of my life since the day my mother took me to see John Wayne's film at the Dixie Drive-In Theatre in Danville, Illinois. I traveled as an "Alamo nut" from the streets and farm fields of Rossville to the halls of Holmes Junior High in Mount Prospect to the graduation stage of Forest View High School and beyond. As affection (or affliction) gave way to profession, and family and friends accepted with shock (and some admiration) the transition, the fascination with the story and the events surrounding it continued. That fascination continues today.

The Alamo is a story borne out of the old Spanish Borderlands, which impacted and transcended the generation that fought for it and the foundries of the nation it helped to create.

With the possible exception of Gettysburg, Pearl Harbor, and the Little Bighorn, the Battle of the Alamo is one of the most famous battles to have occurred on what is now United States soil. An estimated three million visitors a year come to view the remains of this battle site, now dominated by the modern city of San Antonio. Each has his own reasons for making the visit. For some it is merely curiosity, while for others it is a reinforcement of values and beliefs. Some view the Alamo experience as a shining chapter in history, while others prefer to see only the dark shadows of the past and pounce upon the negative. Regardless the reasoning, people do come to the site to remember the Alamo.

Over the years, the Alamo battle has taken on epic proportions. The historical fact, or at least what has been termed as "interpretation" of historical fact, has been fighting a losing battle with legend. Like Lexington, Gettysburg, Masada, Blood River, and Hastings, the Alamo has become one of the defining moments in the birth of a new people and land. It became part of the creation myth process. The men who fought and died there became demi-gods, revered as ones who fell weapons in hand so they could ascend to a Texian Valhalla. The struggle itself, fought over different political ideals, concepts of freedom, national sovereignty, land and perceptions of national destinies, soon became one of "Anglos" vs. "Mexicans."

In the process of the reshaping of the Alamo story as a popular culture landmark, the site itself underwent dramatic changes. By the time Adina De Zavala started her campaigns to save the Alamo, most of the site was long gone. The State of Texas purchased the Alamo church in 1883. But the site was saved not merely to preserve it as a historical landmark or battlefield, but rather to convert the old mission church into a shrine. Since 1903 the Daughters of the Republic of Texas (DRT) have held custodianship of the Alamo buildings, which are owned by the state.

The Daughters, whose patriotic intent has managed to keep the Alamo open to visitors at no cost for nearly 100 years, have often come under fire for their "interpretation" of the "shrine." History groups, activists, politicians, preservationists, and professional troublemakers have all taken swings at the DRT for various lapses in historical interpretation. Mexican-Americans want a "balanced" view; descendants of the Coalition people (who, as Spanish converts, built the Alamo as Mission San Antonio de Valero) want the early history of the site honored. Everyone from the well-intended to commercial exploiters want their piece of the Alamo.

One group which has remained in the shadows of Alamo historiography happens to be the collective with the most connection to the site and the event — the families of the men, women, and children who were present in the Alamo during the famous 1836 siege. Most people assume that the DRT represents these entities. The DRT membership is actually composed of the female descendants of people who resided in Texas from 1821 to 1845. There is also a "Sons" organization with similar membership, but one does not have to have an ancestor who served in the 1835–1836 conflict to qualify.

In fact, many of the DRT and SRT ancestors arrived after Texas independence was achieved. While Alamo descendants who live in Texas may qualify for membership in either organization, the truth is that the Alamo descendants are a distinct minority within this group. A sampling of the DRT Board of Management in 1994–1995 showed only one Alamo descendant. Having an Alamo descendant on the Alamo Committee (the DRT-appointed body that oversees the daily operations of the Alamo) itself is rare. A humorous moment occurred several years ago when a DRT Board of Management member asked a member of the Alamo Defenders Descendants Association (ADDA) what the difference was between the two groups. The ADDA member, with some slight indignance, noted, "Our ancestors actually died here!"

Most Alamo descendants are not historians, although they have developed a strong interest in genealogy. Often they are at odds with historical researchers over the interpretive history of the Alamo battle. Family traditions and the emotion that accompanies them often form a stubborn wall of historical resistance to new research. For years it was assumed that John W. Smith was the last courier out of the Alamo, when in reality it was probably James Allen. A sidebar for historians but near tragedy for one family.

Recently, historian and researcher Thomas Ricks Lindley has been working on a more complete picture of just how many people were in the Alamo. His work, using documents in the Texas State Archives, the General Land Office and the Center for American History, has convinced him that several of the names of Alamo dead on the traditional list are in error. Again, a historical footnote for some, but for the affected families, genealogical trauma.

Another problem has been direct ancestor vs. lineal ancestor. Many people are related to Alamo defenders, but the list narrows when it comes down to direct ancestors. Of course, this is quite apparent when dealing with the Alamo commanders. There are no direct ancestors of James Bowie, although some claim to be. No one bearing the last name of Travis can be traced directly back to William Barret Travis, whose only son died without issue. James Bonham never married, nor produced any recognized heirs. Only David Crockett is left with a large gathering of direct line, who have organized into a wonderful association that meets every other year.

Other Alamo families have also formed associations, but it was not until 1995 that an effort to unite all of the Alamo families was undertaken by Lee Spencer, Pat Jackson, Dorothy Perez, Ray Esparza, and Francis John. The organization formed in the middle of yet another battle between rival groups over what direction the development of Alamo Plaza should take. Paramount in this issue was the closure of Alamo Plaza East out of respect for the abandoned *campo santo* (burial ground) of the Valero/Alamo mission. When the City of San Antonio formed a special mayor's committee to discuss these issues, the ADDA requested membership on the panel. The City refused to recognize the organization, but did allow ADDA representation on one of the subcommittees.

It was remarkable that when such groups as the Inter-Tribal Council of Indians, the Grendaderos de Galvez, and the Alamo Plaza Merchants Association were all allowed representation, the organization that represented descendants of Alamo heroes was not. Eventually, Mayor Nelson Wolff did recognize the ADDA. But his successor, Bill Thorton (one of the principal antagonists on Alamo Plaza development), has not.

The ADDA threw its support behind the Coalition Indian Group in favor of closing the street. This put them at odds with the DRT. But the ADDA strongly stood in favor of continued DRT management of the Alamo during State Representative Gregory Luna's attempt to introduce a bill taking custodianship away from the Daughters. Later, when one of the possible sites of burial of the remains of the Alamo garrison was threatened, the ADDA helped other organizations stop the attack. All of which clearly shows that the descendants of the Alamo are no longer satisfied with remaining in the shadows. The State of Texas, the City of San Antonio, and the DRT are all realizing the Alamo descendants will have a voice in any future Alamo developments.

As a historian, and president of the Alamo Battlefield Association (1994–1996), it has been my great pleasure to see the descendants of the Alamo meet and grow. I was pleased to be asked to be the keynote speaker at their first memorial service inside the Alamo church in 1995, an event which was emotionally overwhelming for all in attendance.

Inside the small building was a unique collection of people from all walks of life: historians, actors, Alamo affectionates, preservationists, DRT and SRT members, descendants of the Coalition Indians who built the place, and, of course, the descendants themselves. A standout moment came when the grandson of Alejo Perez, Jr., the youngest survivor of the battle and the last to die in 1918, stepped to the podium to help give the opening prayer. The spark eliciting emotion was the knowledge that this descendant had been born just early enough to have known as a child his grandfather, an Alamo survivor. The distance of time seemed suddenly much shorter, as there stood a person who knew someone who had been in the 1836 battle. It was as close as most of us would ever be to the people and the event.

Ron Jackson, in putting together *Alamo Legacy*, has had to walk a tightrope between tradition and historical fact. But he was quick to understand that the Alamo descendants do have a voice and it is one that needs to be heard. Regardless of the historical debates over interpretation and fact, the Alamo story is one that still inspires. While the world may claim the Alamo as a symbol, the Alamo descendants claim it as a family would a home or, at best, the family plot in a cemetery. For unlike the rest of us, theirs is not a celluloid or inspirational connection, but one of family blood. It is their legacy.

KEVIN R. YOUNG, President
Alamo Battlefield Association
San Antonio de Bexar
March 6, 1996

Preface

America's gripping saga of the Battle of the Alamo has been told over and over since March 6, 1836. Eyewitnesses, Texas old-timers, newspapers, magazines, television documentaries, movies, writers, and historians have all presented various versions of the epic last stand.

The legend continues to grow today, and is evident by the estimated three million tourists who visit the Alamo annually. But never before has the Alamo story been told in full by the descendants of its participants.

Now, for the first time in 160 years, the Alamo families have been brought together to relive that fateful battle.

Through hundreds of interviews spanning thirty-six states and two countries, I have compiled a unique collection of family legends. Because there is no definitive list of descendants, the hunt for these stories often led to dead ends or only specific branches of a family tree.

In three cases — John McGregor, John Harris, and Henry Warnell — surviving legends are the only proof of a family's ties to an Alamo defender. They have been included until further evidence proves otherwise.

It is my sincere hope that in the coming years more descendants will step forward to tell their family legends.

Each participant connected to the famous siege and battle whose oral history was found has his or her own place in this work. These are the stories passed on by Alamo widows, children of defenders, couriers, scouts, wagon masters, neighbors, and Mexican *soldados*.

In retelling these stories, I have tried to remain true to the family legends and the spirit with which they were told. Memoirs of deceased descendants, letters from defenders and relatives, diaries, family Bibles, and, naturally, oral evidence have all been consulted for this work. Each, I believe, is at the heart of the Alamo legacy.

Segments of various stories will overlap and some will even repeat with different characters taking the lead role. Descendants of couriers James L. Allen and Ben Highsmith, for example, both claim their ancestor was the last to leave the Alamo alive. Descendants of Jose Gregorio Esparza and Francisco Esparza also differ on who received permission from Mexican General Antonio López de Santa Anna to bury Gregorio. Was it Gregorio's wife, Ana, or his brother, Francisco?

Once again, in an effort to preserve each legend, these stories have been presented as told. Each story therefore should stand on its own.

Like many eyewitness accounts, the number of Alamo defenders will also change from story to story. Some repeat the traditional number of 189 men. Others say 200. Or 200-plus. Ultimately, the reader must be the judge.

This work is not intended to be the Bible of Alamo events and participants, but rather a preservation of the oral evidence before it is lost forever. My hope is that this oral evidence will be examined for what it is — oral evidence — and weighed against other historical data.

The history of people should not be confined merely to documented eyewitness accounts, court records, land grants, and death certificates. If that's our definition of history, we as a people need to look in the mirror.

Remembrances of a child's joy or a widow's tears don't always find a way into government reports or museum files. This is where family legends can prove invaluable.

Author Alex Haley left us with perhaps the most profound statement on oral evidence in his epic, historical novel, *Roots*. Haley grew up listening to family stories on his grandma's front porch in Henning, Tennessee. She proudly told him of his African ancestor "Kin-tay," who left his village one day to cut wood for a drum when he was captured by slave traders and hauled off in chains to America.

As an adult, Haley became intrigued by his family's rich oral traditions and sought the knowledge of an African linguistics specialist. Haley learned the words he had heard growing up — "*Ko*" and "*Kamby Bolongo*" — were probably from the "Mandinka" tongue. He would further learn of the West African villages that bore the name of Kinte, and of the old men who lived in these villages called *griots*. These men were literally walking archives of tribal oral histories.

Haley soon found himself journeying to West Africa and into the back-country village of Juffure to visit with one of these fabled *griots*. The old man had recited tribal oral history on the "Kinte" family for about two hours when he stated that roughly between the years of 1750 and 1760, Omoro Kinte and Binta Kinte had four sons — Kunta, Lamin, Suwadu, and Madi.

The old *griot* then noted, "About the time the King's soldiers came, the eldest of these sons, Kunta, went away from his village to chop wood . . . and he was never seen again . . ."

Haley sat frozen as the *griot* continued his narrative. He later wrote of that incredible moment:

> This man who had been in this back-country African village had no way in the world to know that he had just echoed what I had heard all through my boyhood years on my grandma's front porch in Henning, Tennessee . . . of an African who always had insisted that his name was "Kin-tay"; who had called a guitar a "*ko,*" and a river within the state of Virginia, "*Kamby Bolongo*"; and who had been kidnaped into slavery while not far from his village, chopping wood to make himself a drum.[1]

Haley discovered oral traditions can turn historical dates and facts into real events about real people. My hope is that this work will do the same for the story of the Alamo.

While it is inconceivable to think anyone would believe every part of every story in this text, I nonetheless believe this book is dotted with nuggets of truth. May each reader determine for him or herself where those truths lay.

xv

Historians and scholars may be quick to discard this work entirely, citing the many pitfalls of oral evidence — a forgetful great-grandmother, a colorful uncle, etc. But I hope they don't. For within these pages, one will discover real people — the true magic of the Alamo legacy.

Acknowledgments

Chills ran down my back March 5, 1995, in the dimly lit Alamo church. A roll call of the Alamo's defenders was being read, and with each name, descendants quietly rose from their seats to honor their heroic ancestors.

"Juana Navarro de Alsbury . . . Miles DeForest Andross . . . Micajah Autry . . ."

The ceremony marked the 159th anniversary of the famed battle. More importantly, it brought together the families of those who gave their lives for Texas independence for the first time since that tragic Sabbath morning in 1836. The Alamo Defenders Descendants Association was meeting for the first time in its history.

With the announcement of each name, my heart pounded and tears welled in my eyes as I struggled to keep my composure. The emotion of the moment was overwhelming. I couldn't help but feel connected to these people. For in the previous year, many of those in the crowd had warmly let me into their lives and their family's past.

They shared stories, phone numbers, and even family secrets — all because I desired to preserve the written and oral traditions of any family connected to the Alamo battle. Their kindness, like their ceremony, touched my soul.

So with sincere gratitude, I thank every member of the Alamo family. May this book always be their book.

A project such as this can be humbling, especially when you consider there was no definite list of descendants when I began this project in April 1994. I called on "the People of Texas & all

Americans in the World" in my massive hunt for Alamo legends. Many folks throughout the country — and Mexico — came to my aid. There were countless telephone operators, librarians, journalists, and historians who assisted me in my search.

No three people were more helpful, however, than Kevin R. Young, Lee Spencer, and Linda Edwards. Without them, this project simply wouldn't have been completed.

Young, who graciously accepted my offer to write this book's foreword, is the president of the Alamo Battlefield Association and a walking encyclopedia on the Texas Revolution. On many occasions, I called Young to tap his brain for historical tidbits that might give me a better understanding of Texas history. He fielded question after question, never once failing to help this eager writer with an endless appetite for that Texas struggle long ago.

In retrospect, I admire Young as much for his patience as for what he means to the Alamo legacy. He may appear all-business most of the time, but his heart is as big as Texas.

To Spencer, the founding president of the Alamo Defenders Descendants Association, I am equally indebted. She is a woman full of spirit and passion. Over the past two years, she has been a great source of inspiration to me, as well as a dear and trusted friend.

Spencer's great-great-great-great-grandfather Gordon C. Jennings was one of Capt. William R. Carey's "Invincibles," which isn't hard to imagine. Spencer has been my "Invincible" from the start, and was more than willing to share her heart in this book's Introduction.

The Daughters of the Republic of Texas and the Alamo Defenders Descendants Association are lucky to have such a person. For she works for nothing more than the preservation of her heritage, and asks for nothing in return. Sounds like the men of the Alamo.

I am also greatly indebted to the efforts of the DRT Library staff, especially the tireless work of Linda Edwards. She routinely researched files for me while I lived in California, and never failed to dig up the necessary information or drop a kind word of encouragement during our two-year correspondence. Thank you, Linda.

Ed Eakin at Eakin Press in Austin will also never be forgotten. He gave me the opportunity to realize a dream. How many people in our lives can we truly say that about? Much thanks must also go to Eakin editor Melissa Roberts and staff for their careful handling of the manuscript.

Artist Gary Zaboly, whose incredible pen and ink sketches grace this text, must also get three cheers. Zaboly's work simply elevates this book to a higher level, and believe it or not, he's as friendly as his art is good.

Alamo historian and author Bill Groneman was yet another person who graciously offered his time and assistance. Groneman routinely opened his personal files for me without hesitation.

San Antonio Express-News reporter Chris Anderson was also interested enough in my project to devote a Sunday feature to it. The story, which ran over the national wire, focused on my efforts to contact descendants of the Mexican army. Thanks to Anderson, his feature led to three such stories — each a rare find.

I'd also like to thank my grandmother, Nina Bolon, and my great-grandmother, Helen Bolon, for sharing family legends with me. They gave me the idea for this book without even knowing they had.

As this project took flight, I gathered my own group of volunteers. There was friend Dan Reichl, my former city editor who gave this text its first and most difficult reads. He's a Pennsylvanian by birth, but he would have made a good Tennessee Mounted Volunteer. Darlene Giblet also provided some valuable reads and the insightful comments of an avid reader. There was Al LaGardo, a close friend and noted California boxing trainer, who served as my Mexican interpreter. And there was Joy Hanek, who chipped in by transcribing tapes. To all, a hearty thanks.

Many people have touched my writing career over the years, starting with my seventh-grade English teacher Kevin Ward. He was the first to encourage me to express my thoughts on paper. Chuck Barney, my first sports editor, took my writing to new heights. Today, I proudly consider myself a protégé of Barney, an award-winning California sports writer.

Others who have touched my career in one way or another are journalists Diane Barney, Cecil Conley, Steve Dempsey,

Steve Harmon, Matt Miller, Tim Roe, Dave Smith, and Greg Trott. California State University–Sacramento professors Joan Moon, Kenneth N. Owens, Peter Shattock, and Karl von den Steinen each furthered my interest in the field of history.

Like the face of the Alamo, there were still others who whispered in my ear. They were Alamo descendants David Esparza (Enrique Esparza), Linda Halliburton (George C. Kimble), George Benavides (Jose Gregorio Esparza), genealogist Gloria Cadena, friend Juanita Luna, my mother and father, and Alan Huffines, author of *No Small Affair*. Their kind words were not forgotten.

Finally, I'd like to thank my wife and children, to whom this book is dedicated. Thanking them is the hardest because thanks isn't enough. They sacrificed much and endured many lonely nights while I rode off to the Alamo.

Through it all, my wife stood by my side, constantly reinforcing my belief in dreams. As for my children, Daddy's trips to San Antonio seemed to go over well as long as I brought back a few toy bowie knives. May this text in some small way inspire them to chase their dreams.

Introduction

One hundred and sixty-plus years have passed since the Alamo walls shook to the concussion of musket and rifle fire. The moment was fleeting for those who laid down their lives for Texas in the Alamo compound, in its long barracks, and within its chapel. Yet the Battle of the Alamo remains as much an inspiration today as it was to 1836 Texians who later defeated Santa Anna's army at San Jacinto with the battle cry "Remember the Alamo!"

Those who fought and died at the Alamo have become legendary heroes. Generations have laid claim to their legacy, the world to their saga. While the Siege and Battle of the Alamo have become many things to many people, for those of us who are direct descendants it is more than just a page in a history book. Or more than merely an inspirational story of courage and self-sacrifice.

When our ancestors shared that moment in time, which was so overpowering and epic, it forever bonded us as an Alamo family. Professors, historians, and architects may argue about the "historical space" or multi-level history of the Alamo grounds. But for us — the bloodline — the sacred soil of the Alamo will always be our family cemetery.

Our families were joined in blood on that cold Sabbath morning, March 6, 1836. Their bodies were burned and their ashes scattered across the ground soaked with their blood.

The garrison clearly fought for the freedom of Texas, thus forming a bridge across cultures and economic status. Whether their name was Fuentes or Brown or unknown, whether they were *Tejano* or African-American or Anglo-Celtic, they were united in the cause. The Alamo heroes are not only symbols of courage, but also of unity.

Now, through their sacrifices, we the descendants have become united through time with a special heritage. We are still a diverse group, spanning many cultures and socio-economic backgrounds. But today we unite, not only to perpetuate the memories of our ancestors but also to preserve historical sites pertaining to the Alamo garrison, its defenders, its couriers, and women and children survivors.

We, naturally, also voice our concerns about the state-owned Alamo grounds and the San Antonio-owned Alamo Plaza, where much defender blood was shed. And we remain active in researching Alamo history, of which much remains a mystery.

Ron Jackson, through his painstaking research and self-sacrificing determination to locate Alamo descendants, has given a voice to the families of the Alamo garrison in this book. We have passed down a rich oral history of the battle and the trials and tribulations of the time between the fall of the Alamo and the victory at San Jacinto. Our story did not end with the Battle of the Alamo.

For six weeks, women and children ran for their lives from the Mexican Army in the "Runaway Scrape," suffering through bitter-cold weather and constant rains. All along, they struggled with an uncertain future. The women and children met their fate with the same courage their husbands and fathers exhibited at the Alamo in order to insure a future for Texas.

The Alamo families were a hardy stock then and continue to be true survivors today.

Many thanks to Jackson for lovingly collecting this oral history so that we might share our stories with you. Through these stories, you will discover that the Alamo heroes are people with whom you can relate. They were ordinary men who performed an extraordinary sacrifice. Some were single men fighting for freedom as their grandfathers had in 1776. Others, like my ancestor Gordon C. Jennings, fought for their home, heart, and family (his being located in nearby Bastrop).

This collection of stories holds a special place in the hearts of the Alamo bloodline, and we are honored to share them. For within each one of us, these stories stir feelings of excitement, sadness, and pride. So the next time you hear "Remember the Alamo!" we hope you remember all the generations who have passed down these colorful and inspiring stories through the years in memory of their loved ones.

God Bless Texas,

MS. LEE NEESE SPENCER
Founding President
Alamo Defenders Descendants
Association

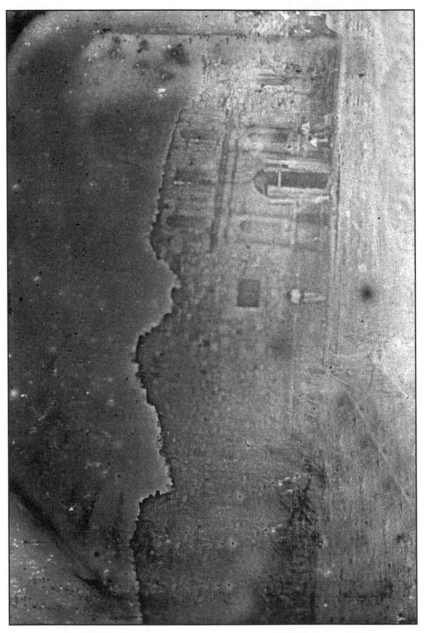

1849 daguerreotype of the Alamo. – Courtesy Center for American History, University of Texas at Austin

PART I

Date with Destiny

March 6, 1836, is a date forever branded in the Texan consciousness. On that day, in the early-morning hours, an estimated 1,800 Mexican *soldados* were hurled at a lonely, frontier mission in Texas called the Alamo which was being defended by some 200 men. To a man, the Texians were wiped out in the onslaught, but not until they had wounded and killed one-third of the Mexicans' assault force.[1]

Immortality in the eyes of Texas would be the only reward for those who made the last stand. Even the Mexicans who participated in the final charge would later speak respectfully of those who gave their lives in defense of the Alamo.

Mexican officer Jose Enrique de la Pena wrote in his diary:

> Death united in one place both friends and enemies; within a few hours a funeral pyre rendered into ashes those men who moments before had been so brave that in a blind fury they had unselfishly offered their lives and had met their ends in combat.[2]

Courageous men on both sides died in this tragedy.

But what has rendered the Alamo story everlasting? Perhaps the same intangible that has made the battles of the Little Bighorn and New Orleans unforgettable snapshots in American history.

What led George Armstrong Custer into the Little Bighorn valley at a time when seven Native American tribes had congregated in one massive campsite which stretched over three miles?[3]

What delivered pirate Jean Lafitte and his band of renegades to the aid of a desperate Andrew Jackson in 1815 as the

1

British attacked New Orleans? And what was Jackson talking about when he declared, "The unerring hand of providence shielded my men,"[4] in the face of so few American casualties?

Destiny. It is a preordained series of events which give historical episodes like the Alamo legendary status.

As with any epic, the Alamo had more than its share of fateful twists and turns before the climactic scene. Numerous family legends tell how various defenders ended up in San Antonio de Bexar just in time to join "Travis, Bowie and Crockett." The ironies seem endless.

Young William T. Malone ran away from his Alabama home and wandered into Texas before ending up at the Alamo. John Henry Dillard traveled to Bexar to sell some grain. And William Wells, Sr., was said to have wandered into Texas thanks to a broken heart.

A number of defenders shared their Texas adventure with family members through letters. With little time to write, and often limited supplies to write with, these men scrawled their hopes and dreams for their loved ones to read about back home. These letters give one the feeling that each man felt destined for something great.

Daniel Cloud, writing to his brother in Kentucky, profoundly stated, "Ever since Texas has unfurled the banner of freedom, and commenced a warfare for liberty or death, our hearts have been inlisted in her behalf."[5]

Capt. William R. Carey boasted to his family in Baltimore about the conduct of his artillery company at the Alamo. Carey dubbed his troops "The Invincibles," and even quipped in a letter, "To relate circumstances of their bravery it would fill a large book."[6]

Carey and Cloud both believed they had a date with destiny.

Soldiers in the Mexican Army were hardly exempt from this rendezvous with fate. Mexican President-General Antonio López de Santa Anna picked up hundreds of foot *soldados* while traveling northward to Texas. As a few family legends will reveal, the choice to fight wasn't always theirs.

Yet of all who came together for that one fateful moment in time, no one seemed more destined to go down in history at the Alamo than David Crockett.

The former congressman from Tennessee was already celebrated in the United States as a champion of the common man,
as well as the best bear hunter in all the land. Paperback
almanacs portrayed Crockett as a frontier Superman, and he
often played to the mythical role. He once boasted he could "run
faster,-jump higher,-squat lower,-dive deeper,-stay down longer,
-and come out drier, than any man in the whole country."[7]

A folk hero was in the making.

And when Crockett failed to earn re-election to office in
1835, he boldly told his constituents, "You can go to hell, I'm
going to Texas."[8]

Crockett's journey into Texas was chronicled by a number
of newspapers, including some back east. Each step of the way
he was shadowed by his mammoth reputation. On December 11,
1835, the *Albany* (New York) *Journal* reported:

> Colonel Crockett who has recently gone to Texas is probably
> one of the best shots in the world. One hundred men like
> Crockett would be of immense service to the Texians at this
> time — if you could only make them believe that their enemies
> were *bears*, instead of men. Crockett has been known to send a
> rifle ball through the same hole nine times in successive fire.[9]

Everywhere he went, Crockett seemed to add to the legend.
His unique way with words always seemed to win folks over, and
his arrival to Bexar was no different. The forty-nine-year-old
Crockett climbed atop a crate in response to applause by the
Civil Plaza crowd and eloquently stated:

> And fellow citizens, I am among you. I have come to your
> country, though not, I hope, through any selfish motive what-
> ever. I have come to aid you all that I can in your noble cause.
> I shall identify myself with your interests, and all the honor that
> I desire is that of defending as a high private, in common with
> my fellow citizens, the liberties of our common country.[10]

Cheers erupted once again.

By the time Crockett shouldered a rifle at the Alamo, he was
already a living legend. At Fort Defiance in Goliad, some seven-
ty-five miles southeast of Bexar, news of Crockett's presence at
the Alamo was received with much delight.

Volunteer John Sowers Brooks summed up the feeling of many Texians when he wrote in a letter to his father:

> We have just received additional intelligence from Bexar. The Mexicans have made two successive attacks on the Alamo in both of which the gallant little garrison repulsed them with some loss. Probably Davy Crockett "grinned" them off.[11]

Crockett's charismatic personality lives on today, and is evident in numerous family legends handed down by descendants of his fellow defenders. Time and time again, Crockett is a central figure in these stories, reaffirming his legacy as a leader among men.

He was, even then, bigger than life. Such is only fitting, for so were his Alamo comrades and their stories, which follow.

ANDREW J. KENT

Alamo Orphan

Oral evidence for this story was presented by Chester P. Wilkes, who has spent decades preserving Kent family legends. His wife, Doris, is a great-great-great-granddaughter of Alamo defender Andrew J. Kent.

Frightened Mary Ann Kent huddled with her brothers and sisters as they slept on wooden pallets placed atop a dirt floor. Sleep was hard to get, though. All the nine-year-old could hear was the boom of cannon which seemed to rock the Texas prairie.

Time and time again, when all became quiet, a rumble from the cannon blasts would emerge from the ground and echo across the land.

Mary Ann was old enough to know exactly where the roar of the cannon was coming from, and that especially made her scared. For some thirty-five miles away, in an old mission fortress known as the Alamo, a small band of Texians was entrenched in a siege against a large military force of the Mexican Army.

In the Alamo, along with a number of close friends and neighbors, was Mary Ann's father, Andrew Jackson Kent.

The forty-four-year-old Kent had ridden to the aid of the men in the Alamo along with twenty-five others known as the Gonzales Ranging Company of Mounted Volunteers.[12] And now he faced death from the overwhelming numbers in the enemy encampment.

Little Mary Ann had watched and listened as the tension mounted in the months prior to his final departure. She recalled that winter day in 1835 when her father and eighteen-year-old brother, David, rode off to join in the Battle of Gonzales.[13] They would follow the fight into the Siege and Battle of Bexar, where David was slightly wounded.

Andrew Kent took his son, David, home that December after the fighting.

Christmas was a peaceful time in the Kent household. Looking back, Mary Ann often cherished the memory of that holiday at their homestead near the Lavaca River, for that was the last time her family was all together.

David Kent, son of Alamo defender Andrew Jackson Kent.
— Photo courtesy of Chester P. Wilkes

War was now in their lives and there was no turning back. Mexican dictatorship could not be tolerated if they were to make Texas their home.

Everyone in and around Gonzales, including little Mary Ann, knew the Mexican Army would return for revenge.

Settlers had more than the arrival of the Mexicans to worry about, though. Homesteaders also had to guard against the raiding Native Americans in the region. For instance, Indians attacked the Hibbons family east of Gonzales, killing the father and riding off with his wife and two children. Andrew Kent and other men left town in pursuit of the hostile Indians after hearing news of the attack. They returned to town empty-handed, but in time to attend an organizational meeting of the Gonzales Ranging Company of Mounted Volunteers on February 23.

Byrd Lockhart was recruiting men for the ensuing showdown with the Mexican Army. Andrew Kent signed up and added David's name to the list. Two days later, a man rode into Gonzales with news that the Mexican Army had arrived in Bexar and had laid siege to the Texans in the Alamo. A buzz zipped through the tiny town as the newly formed Gonzales Ranging Company made immediate plans to depart for Bexar.

Andrew Kent had another reason to ride out in all haste to join the freedom fighters at the Alamo. By this time, David was back in Bexar.

Mary Ann remembered how terrified the family was at the news of the Mexicans' arrival. She recalled her parents' concerns about David, and how they worried through the night.

The sadness which befell the family when their father rode for Bexar the next morning was another lasting memory.

Neighbors Isaac Millsaps and William E. Summers rode up the Lavaca River early the next morning to pick up Andrew en route to Gonzales. They had a long journey ahead of them. Gonzales was roughly thirty-five miles from the Kent homestead, so the threesome had to travel at a leisurely pace to save the horses.

Heart-wrenching goodbyes were said by everyone before Andrew finally climbed on his horse. As Millsaps, Summers, and Kent started their ride toward Gonzales, Mary Ann heard her father remark, "This time you may see blood."

Mary Ann never saw her father again.

Yet her father's words remained with her for the next eighty years until her death. They haunted her as a little girl listening to cannon on the prairie, and they inspired her throughout her adult life.

Andrew Kent and his two companions reached Gonzales by late afternoon the next day, and by that time, the Gonzales Ranging Company was making arrangements for a meeting place. To Kent's great surprise and relief, he ran into his son.

David Kent had been sent from the Alamo to round up some cattle at a ranch south of Bexar. Upon his return, he had been greeted by the arrival of the Mexican Army. Mexican forces had the Alamo surrounded.

Young Kent was then discovered by Mexican soldiers and had to make a dash for safety. He had eluded the Mexicans and hid in some nearby hills for a day before thinking out his next plan of action. He had decided to return to Gonzales, and as fate would have it, he was reunited with his father.

The reunion turned into an argument the next day.

David wanted to ride back to the Alamo with the Gonzales Ranging Company, while his father insisted on his son returning home. Andrew argued that the family was in danger of both hostile Indians and wandering Mexican soldiers, and that David was needed to lead them to the safety of Gonzales.

On that day, Andrew Kent's word was final.

David returned home and did as his father requested. He delivered the family safely to Gonzales, where they stayed at the house of cousin "Red" Adam Zumwalt. Before leaving for Gonzales, the family drove off the livestock and buried some valuables. Other items deemed of lesser value were simply left behind.

Room was scarce in the family wagon and there weren't enough horses for everyone to ride, so some of the Kent children rode to Gonzales on pack animals.

David came to realize his father had spared his life. Looking back, David couldn't help but believe his father knew they would not return from the Alamo alive.[14]

Andrew Kent never did.

Still, at the time, hopes were high in Gonzales that the men would return. Several families of Alamo defenders converged on the tiny town for protection, and now they shared a common bond.

Even as cannon fire ripped through the night air, the folks in Gonzales clung to hope. So did Mary Ann as she looked up from her bedtime spot on the dirt floor. Her imagination ran wild. Oddly enough, as long as she heard the cannon, she knew there was a chance her father would return home.

Gonzales bustled with action during the day. David and other men who remained in town were talking about riding to the Alamo.

Scout Erastus "Deaf" Smith was hurriedly attempting to rally some men together, and David was more than willing to ride. David's friend, Ben Highsmith, was among those ready to ride at a moment's notice. Highsmith had just returned from the Alamo, where he encountered the same problem David did days earlier. Highsmith was delivering a letter from Col. James Fannin at Goliad to Lt. Col. William Barret Travis at the Alamo when he discovered the garrison's thorny problem. From high atop Powder House Hill, Highsmith saw the Alamo surrounded by Mexican forces. He was then spotted by Mexican cavalrymen and chased for about six miles before finally escaping to Gonzales.[15]

David Kent and Highsmith now waited with "Deaf" Smith and others. They expected more men to arrive from the eastern settlements ready to engage the Mexican Army.

A few volunteers straggled into town, but not enough to ride for the Alamo. Anxiously, they waited.

Cannon blasts shattered the silence of the prairie on the morning of March 6.

Mary Ann, drowsy from sleep, awoke to the boom of the cannon from Zumwalt's dirt floor around 3:00 A.M. The cannon fire was constant for roughly three hours before the prairie fell silent.

A signal gun from the Alamo was supposed to go off at noon and again at sunset to indicate the garrison was still in the hands of the Texians. But on this day, there was only silence. The people in Gonzales feared the worst.

Some men rode closer to Bexar to see if they could hear any gunfire. They heard none.[16]

Five days passed, and on March 11, Gen. Sam Houston rolled into Gonzales. Speculation of the Alamo's fall bombarded Houston as he tried to compile some solid evidence on the status of the men in Bexar. David Kent saw the general and brought him Highsmith, who turned over the letter from Fannin he had attempted to carry to Travis. Highsmith retold the story of his narrow escape to the general.

Houston read the letter and immediately wrote Fannin. The general then dispatched Kent and Highsmith to carry his message to Fannin at Goliad. After Kent notified his family of his destination, he and his friend hurriedly rode out.

Shortly after the departure of Kent and Highsmith, Anselmo Borgara and Andres Barcena wandered into Gonzales with the horrifying news of the Alamo's fall. Houston arrested both for spreading false rumors.

"Deaf" Smith and others returned to Gonzales with more inconclusive news. Smith told the general he had been on a hill above the Alamo and had seen no activity.[17]

All reports became obsolete when a haggard and distraught Susanna Dickinson arrived in Gonzales with a firsthand account of the Alamo's dreadful defeat. Dickinson said every man, including her husband, Capt. Almeron Dickinson, was killed in the slaughter.

Andrew Kent, Isaac Millsaps, William E. Summers, George Kimble . . . all were killed. No man was spared.

The nightmarish details struck fear and panic into the people of Gonzales, and sparked what became known as the Runaway Scrape. Families scurried to round up their belongings and fled toward the eastern settlements. The Kents joined in the exodus.

The family had no wagon or cart. They didn't even have enough horses for everyone to ride, so some members walked or led pack animals. Mary Ann remembered giving out from exhaustion. She was placed on a pack horse.

Rain, wind, and frost beat at the Kents as they camped on the open prairie for the next several weeks. Two daughters of Zumwalt, Elizabeth and Eli Mitchell, died on the arduous journey. Both were younger than two. Mary Ann and the rest of the

Kents, meanwhile, continued to mourn the loss of their brave father.

Wildflowers blossomed across the countryside as the sun replaced the rainy skies. Mary Ann remembered walking through those beautiful wildflowers for days. And like those wildflowers, so bloomed a new day in Texas. Freedom was finally won April 21 when Texian forces defeated the main body of the Mexican Army at the Battle of San Jacinto.

The Kent family did not return to Lavaca County until the spring of 1837 to plant crops. Like most of their neighbors, they returned to charred, gutted-out houses. Yet they never lost their pioneering spirit. And they never forgot their father's contributions.

Eight decades later, Mary Ann lived in a log cabin on the banks of the Guadalupe River and received many visitors who wished to learn more of the Texas Revolution. Although she was growing blind and deaf, "Grandma Morriss," as she became known, always shared her thrilling tales. Carrying on the legacy of her heroic father and others who fought for Texas independence was the least she could do.

Mary Ann had refused to give up her simple lifestyle at the log cabin. If a log cabin was good enough for Andrew Kent to die for, she often said, it was good enough for her to live in.

Mary Ann Kent Morriss died February 24, 1917, at the age of eighty-nine.

In 1932, Mary Ann's crumbling log cabin was washed away by a flood. Texas, on the other hand, stood strong and free.[18]

JOHN HENRY DILLARD

Granny's Stories

Susan Alice Cargile presented the oral evidence for this story. Cargile is a great-great-granddaughter of Alamo defender John Henry Dillard, and heard many stories about her famous ancestor from Dillard's daughter, Susan Dillard Hickey.

Susan Dillard Hickey. Folks simply called her "Granny Hickey," and for a woman who weighed all of eighty pounds and measured no higher than five feet, she stood mighty tall to those who remembered her.

Granny Hickey's legacy is somewhat bigger than life in family legends, which shouldn't really come as a shock to anyone. After all, she was a Texan — and no words could ever describe her pride in that fact.

She first arrived in Texas shortly after the Texas Revolution. She was there when Texas became part of the United States. She was there for the dawning of the twentieth century. And she was there when she lived out her final days in peace at her daughter's home in the town of Comanche.

Hair parted down the middle and tied behind her head in a tight knot, Granny Hickey was a picture of family strength and endurance. This woman, who had survived everything from Indian raids to the Civil War, had eyes which always seemed to sparkle just beyond her wire-rimmed glasses.

Granny Hickey often spent her afternoons on the front porch easing back and forth on her rocking chair. Friends and family would come from all over to visit with her, and when she spoke, all listened. She was a living history book.

From time to time, for those lucky enough to be in her presence, she would tell the story which was perhaps closest to her heart. Granny Hickey would talk about her father, John Henry Dillard.

Granny Hickey was born August 6, 1831, in Dyer County, Tennessee, and she barely got to know her father before he left for the wide open territory of Texas in 1835. Like many fellow Americans, Dillard was in search of a new beginning for himself and his family.

Dillard was convinced the Mexican province of Tejas held all the answers to a new, fruitful life. So he set off on an adventurous journey with his close friend, "Uncle" Sutherland Mayfield.

Both men arrived in Texas as planned, and with Dillard's persuasion, settled on a piece of land in Robertson Colony near Washington-on-the-Brazos.

By January of 1836, both men were beginning to see the fruits of their labor. Dillard was harvesting his first grain crop and Sutherland had a new lot of oxen. These fortuitous conditions led the two men to load up the grain and head for Bexar on a trading trip.

Dillard and Sutherland arrived in Bexar sometime in late February. Bexar was the hot spot of the revolution with Mexico, and Dillard and Sutherland quickly learned they were indeed in dangerous territory.

A faction of the Texas Army, heavily consisting of volunteers, had already moved into the Alamo in preparation for the expected Mexican counterattack. Dillard's grain was desperately needed by the Texas forces as they continued to fortify themselves for the next battle.

Dillard was entertaining the idea of joining the soldiers in arms. Freedom, Dillard thought, was worthy of any price.

Then, in all the commotion, Dillard ran into an old friend from Tennessee, the famed David Crockett. They had been neighbors back home, and the two talked for a long time about the events swirling around Bexar.

Dillard told Crockett he was sympathetic to the situation, and after some careful thought, he said he would stay and fight. Sutherland remained in Bexar until he could make up his mind to stay or leave.

The presence of the Mexican Army helped Sutherland come to a speedy decision. He would leave.

Dillard respected Sutherland's decision, and asked his close friend to take care of his family back in Tennessee should anything happen to him. Sutherland agreed and left the Alamo, barely slipping out the east side of the town.

On March 6, 1836, Dillard died along with 200 other Texians fighting for freedom against the vast Mexican forces of 5,000.

"Uncle" Sutherland, meanwhile, remained true to his word. He returned to Tennessee upon hearing of his friend's heroic death, and took care of Dillard's wife and children. In fact, "Uncle" Sutherland did such a good job, he married Dillard's widow, Sarah, and moved them to Texas.

At the age of six, Granny Hickey moved from Tennessee to Texas along with her mother, brother, stepfather and his nine children. They traveled by covered wagon, never forgetting Dillard's heroic deed.[19]

WILLIAM T. MALONE

The Runaway

*The following story about Alamo defender William T. Malone is based
on a document on file in the district court of Parker County, Texas.
The document is a compilation of family recollections.*

Thomas Hill Malone and his wife, Elizabeth, eagerly awaited the arrival of the messenger they sent to Texas. Or did they
actually dread the moment?

The confusion was easy to understand.

Thomas sent the messenger to Texas to inquire the fate of
their eldest son, William Thomas, who left home in the fall of
1835. The Malones heard a short time later that William was one
of those slain March 6, 1836, in defense of the Alamo in Bexar.

News of William's death deeply saddened the family, especially Elizabeth, who had been sick over her son's sudden departure from their Alabama home. She had received a letter from
William shortly after he left home, and hadn't heard from him
again.

The reports coming out of Texas weren't promising.

Word was there were no survivors except a Mrs. Dickinson
and her baby. But rumors and reports weren't good enough for
Thomas Malone and his family. They needed to know more.

William's exodus for Texas was the source of much pain for
the Malone family. No one liked to talk about his departure, although everyone did. The story was especially painful for his
father.

Thomas was a pious Methodist, unflinching in his beliefs,
and William was often his opposite. The eighteen-year-old William was an outgoing, handsome young man. He had the dark-
est complexion in the family, nearly black hair, and was rather
large for his age. All his schoolmates feared him for he was
always a head taller and known for his excessive courage.

William also had an addiction for socializing, gambling, and
drinking. Naturally, his father didn't approve of his lifestyle.

One time William stumbled home drunk and his father was
enraged. Thomas Malone was embarrassed by his son's behav-

ior. He warned William never again to come home in such a drunken state or he would pay dearly for his foolishness.

William took his father seriously.

Unfortunately for everyone involved, William had another encounter with the bottle. Instead of facing the wrath of his Bible-thumping father, the wayward William hopped on a horse and rode for Texas.

Thomas followed his son all the way to New Orleans in hopes of retrieving him, but was disappointed to learn he was too late. William, he was told, had moved on to Texas. Thomas knew he would have to return home to a weeping wife.

A lack of finality still remained with the Malones despite reports of William's death. The uncertainty seemed to eat at their souls. Thus, they waited anxiously for the messenger's return.

The messenger put their souls at ease.

While in Texas, the messenger called on Alamo survivor Susanna Dickinson. She was very informative and remembered a young man named Malone in her husband, Almeron's, mess. Malone, she recalled, was only in the Alamo for a short time before it was overtaken by the Mexican Army.

Mrs. Dickinson told the messenger the young Malone died bravely, fighting like a man to the bitter end.

In a way, the Malones were relieved. At least the reports were confirmed by someone who was there. Still, the pain lingered until their deaths.

Elizabeth Malone clutched the letter William had sent her and carried it with her at all times until it wore out.[20]

Elizabeth had strong feelings about the bounty of Texas land the Malone family was entitled to for William's service. Family members often heard her firmly state, "I never want to own a foot of that land. I want it left for the wild beasts to roam over, because it was bought with the blood of my child."[21]

RUIZ

Mistreated Soldado

Oral evidence for the following story was presented by Frances Araiza, who was a little girl when told about her ancestor in Santa Anna's army. She heard the story from her grandmother, Demetria Ruiz. Unfortunately, the first name of the Mexican soldado *has been lost in the story's descent.*

Ruiz was only a boy when he witnessed the fall of the Alamo on March 6, 1836. He was a conscripted *soldado* in the Mexican Army, and descendants remember being told he was no older than fifteen when drafted into service.

He was forced to join the Mexican Army in the winter of 1836, when General Santa Anna and his troops marched into San Luis Potosi. Mexican officers knocked door-to-door in search of prospective foot *soldados,* and when they reached the Ruiz household, they added one more name to their ever-growing force.

Ruiz often commented on how poorly the troops were treated. He, for one, had to walk all the way from San Luis Potosi into the Mexican province of *Tejas.* Any *soldados* who complained or stopped to rest were shot on the spot.

Ruiz and other foot *soldados* often tried to help carry fellow recruits who were groggy from exhaustion. Some weren't so lucky. Ruiz saw several *soldados* stumble and fall from exhaustion, only to be instantly executed by unsympathetic officers.

Eating was another miserable experience. Over smoldering charcoal, meat was cooked briefly on one side and then flipped over and roasted for the same amount of time. The end result was a bloody, nearly raw piece of steak for each *soldado.*

Ruiz's reward for his long, grueling journey was war, where he survived the carnage of the Alamo.

At some point after the defeat of Texian forces at Bexar, Ruiz escaped the Mexican Army. He was fed up with being mistreated.

Thus ended the military career of one boy foot *soldado.*

Ruiz eventually settled in Texas, where his descendants live today.[22]

MICAJAH AUTRY

A Daughter Remembers

Details for the following passage are based on Mary Autry Greer's written account of her father, Micajah Autry, who rode into the Alamo with the group that became popularly known as the Tennessee Mounted Volunteers. The letters are those written by Autry to his wife, Martha, who was back home in Jackson, Tennessee.

Mary Autry Greer grew to savor every memory of her father, Micajah Autry — his rich, tenor voice, his poems, his sketches, his graceful equestrian skills. No detail was too small to cherish. Each and every memory was sweet, for she was only a little girl when he died.

Word of his death came to Mary on the most beautiful of April mornings in 1836. As she frolicked outside her log home with a playmate, gathering white and pink flowers from dogwoods in blossom, a voice shattered the serenity of the Autry yard in Jackson, Tennessee.

"You must come to the house," the voice cried out to Mary. "Your father has been killed and your mother half dead with the news."

Mary would later write, "Breathless I ran and was greeted with choking sobs as she tried to tell me the tragic news."

In time, Mary heard the whole story. Her loving father, who had ventured to Texas in search of land and a new beginning for his family, had joined the revolution against Mexico.

Micajah had stood side-by-side with the celebrated David Crockett — a fellow Tennessean — and had died a heroic death March 6, 1836, in defense of the Alamo. "Neither of them I think anticipated war," Mary later wrote, "but instantly volunteered and were sent by the overland road to the defense of 'The Alamo.'"

Texas first called to Micajah while he was on business trips to Philadelphia and New York. He and a law partner were going to make their fortune in the mercantile business, but instead caught wind of Stephen F. Austin's colonies in Texas. Micajah figured he would give Texas a try, and he hit the trail in 1835.[23]

The Autrys would track his journey to Texas through the letters he sent home. The first letter was dated Memphis, Tennessee, December 7, 1835. Micajah wrote:

> I have taken my passage in the steamboat Pacific and shall leave in an hour or two. . . . I have met in the same boat a number of acquaintances from Nashville and the District, bound for Texas, among whom are George C. Childress and his brother. Childress thinks the fighting will be over before we get there, and speaks cheeringly of the prospects. I feel more energy than I ever did in anything I have undertaken. I am determined to provide for you a home or perish. . . . Fare you all well till you hear from me again, perhaps from Natchez. . . .[24]

In a December 13, 1835, letter from Natchitoches, Autry wrote:

> About 20 minutes ago I landed at this place safely after considerable peril. About 20 men from Tennessee formed our squad at Memphis, and all landed safely at the mouth of Red River. Major Eaton and Lady were on board the Pacific, to whom I suppose I was favourably introduced by Mr. Childress, from that however or from some other reason Gov. Eaton paid me the most friendly and assiduous attention. . . . I have not met with a more amiable and agreeable man than the Governor. By his persuasion a Major Arnold from Tennessee (a cousin of Gen'l Arnold) and myself left the rest of our Company at the mouth of Red River and went down to Orleans for the purpose of learning the true state of things in Texas as well as which would be the best probable rout. The result was that, the war is still going on favourably to the Texans, but it is thought that Santa Anna will make a descent with his whole forces in the Spring, but there will be soldiers enough of the real grit in Texas by that time to overrun all Mexico.
>
> The only danger is in starvation, for the impulse to Texas both as to soldiers and moving families exceeds anything I have ever known. I have little doubt but that the army will receive ample supplies from Orleans both of provisions and munitions of war, as the people of Texas have formed themselves into something like a government, which will give them credit in Orleans. I have had many glowing descriptions of the country by those who have been there. . . . We have between

400 and 500 miles to foot it to the seat of government, for we cannot get horses, but we have sworn allegiance to each other and will get along somehow. . . . The smallpox has recently broken out here very bad, but I fear the Tavern bill a great deal worse. Such charges never heard of and we have to stay here probably several days before we can procure a conveyance for our baggage. I suppose we shall join and buy a waggon.

Write to me to this place all the letters you send by mail, perhaps the general intercourse from here to Texas, will enable me to get them conveniently. Write me in Texas by every private opportunity, and I will do the same. . . . I send this by Mr. Sevier who promises to put it in the postoffice at Bolivar or Middleburg. . . .

P.S. The Company of young men that left Jackson before I did passed through here about 20 days ago.[25]

Autry would write one last time from Texas just prior to his final march to Bexar. The letter follows:

Nacogdoches, Jany. 13th, 1836

My Dear Martha,

I have reached this point after many hardships and privations but thank God in most excellent health. The very great fatigue I have suffered has in a degree stifled reflection and has been an advantage to me. I walked from Nachitoches whence I wrote you last to this place 115 miles through torrents of rain, mud and water. I had remained a few days in St. Augustine when Capt. Kimble from Clarksvelle, Ten. a lawyer of whom you may recollect to have heard me speak arrived with a small company of select men, 4 of them lawyers. I joined them and find them perfect gentlemen. We are waiting for a company daily expected from Columbia, Ten. under Col. Hill with whom we expect to march to head quarters (Washington) 125 miles from here, where we shall join Houston the commander in chief and receive our destination. I may or may not receive promotion as there are many very meritorious men seeking the same. I have become one of the most thorough going men you ever heard of. I go the whole Hog in the cause of Texas. I expect to help them gain their independence and also to form their civil government, for it is worth risking many lives for.

From what I have seen and learned from others there is not so fair a portion of the earth's surface warmed by the sun.

Be of good cheer Martha I will provide you a sweet home. I shall be entitled to 640 acres of land for my services in the army and 4444 acres upon condition of settling my family here. Whether I shall be able to move you here next fall or not will depend upon the termination of the present contest. Some say that Santa Ana is in the field with an immense army and near the confines of Texas, others say since the conquest of St. Antonio by the Texians and the imprisonment of Genl' Cos and 1100 men of which you have no doubt heard, that Santa Ana has become intimidated for fear that the Texians will drive the war into his dominions and is now holding himself in readiness to fly to Europe which latter report I am inclined to discredit, what is the truth of the matter no one here knows or pretends to know.

Tell Mr. Smith not to think of remaining where he is but to be ready to come to this country at the very moment the government shall be settled, as for a trifle he may procure a possession of land that will make a fortune for himself, his children and his children's children of its own increase in value and such a cotton country is not under the sun. I have just been introduced to Mr. McNiell a nephew of Mr. S. who is now in this place and appears to be much of a gentleman. Give my most kind affection to Amelia and Mr. Smith and to my own Dear Mary and James give a thousand tender embraces and for you my Dearest Martha may the smile of heaven keep you as happy as possible til we meet.

M. Autry.

Tell Brothers J. & S. I have not time to write to them at present as Mr. Madding and Sevier by whom I send this can not wait. Tell Brother Jack to think of nothing but coming here with us; that if he knew as much about this country as I already do he would not be kept from it. Tell him to study law as this will be the greatest country for that profession as soon as we have a government that ever was known.

M.A.

P.S. We stand guard of nights and night before last was mine to stand two hours during which the moon rose in all her mildness but splendor and majesty. With what pleasure did I contemplate that lovely orb chiefly because I recollected how often you and I had taken pleasure in standing in the door and contemplating her together. Indeed I imagined that you might be looking at her at the same time. Farewell Dear Martha.

M.A.

P.S. Col. Crockett has just joined our company.[26]

Less than two months later, Autry would lie dead along with the rest of the Alamo's defenders. Family legend would later claim Autry fell near Crockett and the wooden palisade they helped defend on the southern end of the garrison, but in truth, no one is sure what happened in the tragic melee.

Autry descendants are satisfied he died an honorable death.

Of this, Mary was certain. She may have felt cheated by the childhood loss of her father, but if so, never recorded her feelings. Instead, she seemed to have been overwhelmed by pride.

"My father was a man in word and deed, in action as well as profession," Mary would write. "Peace to his memory, says his one remaining child and I believe the millions (who) now claim Texas (beautiful Texas) as home, will answer, 'Amen!' "[27]

DANIEL W. CLOUD

Death in the Cause of Liberty

Oral evidence for the following passage was presented by Pat Cloud, who collects family history. Her husband, Robert, is Alamo defender Daniel W. Cloud's great-great-nephew. The letters are those written by Cloud to his family in Logan County, Kentucky.

Family members passed Daniel W. Cloud's letter around freely after its arrival in Logan County, Kentucky. Cloud's travels into Louisiana and the adventures which awaited him in Texas stirred both excitement and fear within each family member.

He wrote of the country he had passed, of the brilliant prospects for settlement and of joining the Texas Revolution. The news was enthralling.

Word of Cloud's letter had spread like wildfire throughout

Logan County since he left in October with fellow residents B. Archer M. Thomas, Peter J. Bailey, William Keener Fauntleroy, and Joseph G. Washington.

John B. Cloud was especially gripped by the letter since it was addressed to him from his beloved brother. He wondered. He worried. He hoped. But that was months ago, and now the letter had taken on a whole new meaning of importance for John.

Daniel had been killed.

John B. Cloud was told his brother died March 6, 1836, in Bexar in a military engagement with the Mexican Army.[28] Since then, he had often thought of that cherished letter and the words echoed in his head.

> Near Natchitoches, La.
> December, 26th, 1835

Beloved Brother:

A long time has elapsed since we parted and long before this period, I expected to write you, but continual traveling and employment have prevented. After leaving Uncle Sloan's in Missouri which we did on the 29th of November, we journeyed South. I left the family well except Grandma, who was extremely ill. I have no idea that she yet lives. I left upwards of $30.00 with her besides the $10.00 sent her by Uncle William, which made forty and fifty dollars, which I deem sufficient in the event of life or death. She had blankets and every kind of comfortable clothing and all that Aunt could do to alleviate her suffering was done. We set off before Aunt Rice and her family arrived, but were informed that they had good health and enough to eat and wear.

Now you wish me to say something of the country through which we have traveled, Viz, Illinois, Missouri, Arkansas and Louisiana.

The soil of Ill. North of 38 degrees is the best I ever saw and from all I can learn, the best body of land on earth of the same extent. The water is abundant and may be called good, many parts I regard as healthy, and the ridgeland between Ill. and the Mississippi River, I believe to be as healthful as the allegany mountains.

Yankees, Kentuckians and Ohion's etc., are filling up the

State with a rapidity unparalled in the History of the West. I saw as fine Farms, good houses, barns, wagons, plows, horses, men, women, children, beds, tables, and furniture in Ill. as I ever saw in Ky. I view this State at no distant day far in advance of any western State except Ohio.

The reasons which induced us to travel on, were briefly these, First our curiosity was unsatisfied, second, Law Dockets were not large, fees low, and yankee lawyers numerous, Third the coldness of the Climate. Missouri, like Ill. has too much praries and unlike her, has very poor praries, West of 15 degrees, west longitude from Washington city, the lands of both sides of the Mo. River about the depth of one County, including Boon, Howard, Carroll, Ray, Clay, and Clinton on the North, and Cooper, Saline, LaFayette, Jackson, VanBuren, etc on the South are very rich and well settled already.

Our reason for not stopping in Mo. were first we were disappointed in the face of the country and the coldness of the climate, but most of all the smallness of the docket. There is less litigation in this State than in any other State in the Union, for its population as I was informed, by one of the Judges of the Supreme Court, Judge Tomkins, and what is going on redounds very little to the emolument of the practitioner. I was happy to find such a State of case existing, but while following chase like other hunters, wish to go where game is plentiful, large and fat, we rode through Mo., from North to South, about six hundred miles the weather was growing cold we knew we could not settle, it was out of our way to go through boonville and we had not an opportunity to presenting ourselves to Col. Boon and Mr. Grubbs, but we thank Brother Grubbs, for the letter of introduction which he gave us and which we yet keep.

We wish you to acquaint him with these facts, and to present our love and compliments to him and his family.

We found Ark. Territory, in some places rich, well watered, and healthy and society tolerably good, but the great body of the country is stony sandy and mountainous. In passing through we traveled ten days constantly in crossing the Mountains. On Red River the lands are immensely rich, and planters also many of them worth two hundred and three hundred thousand dollars, had we chosen to locate in Ark. we would have made money rapidly, if blessed with health and life. Dockets and Fees being large. The reason for our pushing still further on, must now be told and as it is a Master one, it will suffice without the mention of any other. Ever since Texas has unfurled the banner of freedom, and commenced a warfare for liberty or death, our hearts have been inlisted in her behalf. The progress of her cause has increased the ardor of our feelings until we have resolved to embark in the vessel which contains the flag of Liberty and sink or swim in it's defense.

Our Brethren of Texas were invited by the Mexican Government, while Republican in it's form to come and settle, they did so, they have endured all the privations and sufferings incident to the settlement of a frontier country, and have surrounded themselves with all the comforts and conveniences of life. Now the Mexicans, with unblushing effrontery call on them to submit to a Monarchial Tyranical, Central despotism, at the bare mention of which every true hearted son of Ky. feels an instinctive horror, followed by a firm and steady glow of virtuous indignation.

The cause of Philanthropy, of Humanity, of Liberty and human happiness throughout the world, called loudly on every man who can to aid Texas.

If you ask me how I reconcile the duty of a soldier with those of a Christian, I refer you to the memorable conversation between Col. Marion and DeKalb, on this point, and the sentiments of the latter I have adopted as my own.

If we succeed, the Country is ours. It is immense in extent, and fertile in its soil. and will amply reward all our toil. If we fail, death in the cause of liberty and humanity is not cause for shuddering. Our rifles are by our side, and choice guns they are, we know what awaits us, and are prepared to meet it.

My Dear Brother, I am in the hands of the omnipotence and rejoice in the hope of his favor and protection. Oh how I would have rejoiced to receive a letter from some of you in Jefferson City in compliance with the request I made in my letter from Springfield, Ill.

I waited ten days and nothing came. I have not heard one sylable from home since the day of our departure.

I now say again if you or any of our relatives will write to us and direct your letters to Nachitoches, La., we may get them, and would thank you most sincerely for them. If you have any affection for us you will attend this request, I now commission you to bear me as a Son, as an affectionate Son, to my beloved Mother and her husband, kiss Sister and all the children for me, Mr. Slack and Mr. Lewis must do the same with their children, to Uncle Samuel and William, and their families, remember me and inform them to Grandma's condition.

Dear Brother, we are of the same origin, the blood of the same Parents flows through our veins, and the same material tenderness watched over our infant slumbers, and the same councils instilled principles into our minds.

Many times have we slept the live long night locked in each others arms. May our united petitions to a throne of divine grace invoke the same bread of life and our souls united in love, finally nestle under the protecting shield of the same all-wise and all merciful redeemer.

Remember me to all the Brethren and acquaintances, who inquire and say to them that scarcety of paper prevents me from writing them personally.

We cannot go to Nachitoches for paper on account of the Small pox. In a few days we shall be in Texas and then having no means of writing you may not hear from us for many days, but when we can, we will write. The deed I made you on the 20th day of October for the 64½ acres of land, is hereby confirmed.

Request Uncle Samuel, to inform Dr. Fishback by letter that he has his books, some of you must take the trouble of informing me at length of all that has occurred in Logan County. I am extremely anxious to hear.

Tell Brother Isham to write. I will sometime write to Brother Anderson, tell him I think well of the country about Quincy, Ill. I think he will be pleased if not too cold for him. My health has been tolerably good. I have suffered a great deal with my stomach, but am now considerable improved.

I hope I shall recover entirely the hardships I am destined to undergo. Mr. Bailey has fine health, we have been traveling ten weeks, and have gone over about twenty five hundred miles.

If I were with you, I could talk enough to tire you. I hope we shall meet.

Your Brother,
D.W. Cloud[29]

As the years passed, John B. Cloud and his family often recalled that day in 1835 when Daniel departed for Texas. He was excited about the trip, and upon final inventory of his gear, realized in the rush of the moment he left his gun in the house.

Daniel sent his niece, Clarissa Cloud, back into the house to retrieve his gun.

As fate would have it, Daniel Cloud really needed little else for his journey.[30]

WILLIAM P. KING

Family Bible

Minnie Shelton presented the oral evidence for the following story of Alamo defender William P. King. Shelton, a great-niece of King, heard the story from her grandmother, Minnie Foster.

Dust swirled upward from the thundering thud of the horses' hooves in front of the King homestead, which sat some fifteen miles north of Gonzales. Men jumped down from their horses in a hurry and approached the family members as they started to gather outside on a cold March morning in 1836.

John G. King, the father of the household, was the first to greet the men. Firm handshakes were issued all around, as were sincere looks of concern.

Everyone knew this wasn't a social visit.

The group was the Gonzales Ranging Company, and they were riding in all haste to aid the men at the Alamo garrison in Bexar. Reliable word was that the Alamo was surrounded by a large force of the Mexican Army.

Relief was needed at once, and those near Gonzales felt especially patriotic in answering the call. If their neighbors and fellow countrymen fell in battle, they could very easily be next.

The choice was rather simple. They would fight for their families, their homes, their freedom and their new country.

Each member of the Gonzales Ranging Company, however, knew deep down the chances of returning home were slim or none. Nonetheless, King wanted to be counted among the volunteers.

King climbed aboard his horse and looked down at his wife, Parmelia. He again glanced at his children — nine in all — and said his final farewells.

Just then, King's eldest son, William, grabbed his reins.

"Please don't go," William begged his father. "You are need-ed at home. Let me go in your place."

Pride swelled in the elder King, who hesitantly agreed to his son's wishes. Perhaps it was the best decision for the entire family.

William promptly hopped on the horse and rode off with the company of volunteers. His family would never see him again.[31]

The selfless act of William P. King has since been celebrat-ed by generations of kin, who continue to retell his heroic story. The final chapter of his life was handwritten into a cherished family Bible, which had been published in 1824.

A notation in the dusty Bible discloses his fate. The Bible reads: "William Phillip King was killed in defense of the Alamo on the 6th day of March 1836 and was aged 16 years 4 months 28 days."[32]

WILLIAM R. CAREY

Dear Brother & Sister

Capt. William R. Carey of the Alamo garrison wrote the letter in the following passage to his brother and sister on January 12, 1836, from Bexar. The letter was addressed to his brother-in-law, William F. Op-pelt, and shipped out of Natchitoches, Louisiana, February 7, 1836.

Title to James Polk's land in Texas was being challenged in 1861. The Baltimore native had purchased the land from Moses T. Carey, who sold Polk a portion of the prairie soil he received as bounty for his son's service in the Texas Revolution.

Carey's son, William R., was a captain of artillery at the Ala-mo. He died along with the other heroic men of that garrison on March 6, 1836. Those who knew the Careys were well acquaint-ed with the last-stand story.

So when Polk's land title was under fire, he went to Carey's family to help secure his claim. Carey's sister provided Polk a letter which had been written by her brother from the Alamo January 12, 1836.

The letter, now a family heirloom, was copied word for word by Polk and sent to his Texas attorney in San Antonio. Thanks in part to the letter, Polk retained title to the land.

St. Antonio De Bexar
Jan. 12, 1836

Dear Brother & Sister

To give you any satisfaction about my situation at present I should have to give you a history of Texas and the Mexican Government, but let me commence by saying that I am in the volunteer army of Texas. I arrived at Washington on the 28th of July. This is a small town situated on the Brazos river & there I intended to take up my final residence, but the unsettled state of affairs between Texas & the Mexican Government, I was called to the field. Movements on the part of the Mexicans aroused our suspicions. They want to establish Centralism or rather military despotism, a government that is repugnant to the principals of free born Americans, we remonstrated and sent commissioners, but we could not positively ascertain on account of their treachery and deceit. They denied it and still they were making preparations for it, but we were on the alert. I shall have to state the situation of this place [Bexar] and also the town of Gonzales so as to give a little information on the affair. This place is an ancient Mexican fort & Town divided by a small river which eminates from Springs. The town has two Squares in and the church in the centre, one a military and the other a government square. The Alamo or the fort as we call it, is a very old building, built for the purpose of protecting the citizens from hostile Indians. The Mexican army or rather part of them came to this place commanded by Martin de Perfecto de Coss, a bold aspiring young General. The town of Gonzales is about 78 miles below this place on the Warloupe [Guadalupe] river. The enemy (as I shall now call them) sent about 200 of their troops to Gonzales after a cannon that they sent there for the use of the citizens to fight the indians. We then were aroused and watched closely their movements. Volunteers was called for to fight for their country I was one of the first that started, about 150 of us ready in a moments warning, and we marched to Gonzales and put the enemy to flight they retreated to this place, we then considered it essentially necessary for the security of our peace to drive them from this place, but we concluded to wait for reinforcements as we were so few in number, and they in a fortified place but unfortunately for us they commenced fortifying the town and strengthing the alamo until it became almost impossible to overcome them, our number increased gradually to the amount of 800 but on account of so many office seekers there was nothing but confussion, contention and discord throughout the encampment, which was within a half a mile of the place, for we came up to endeavor to starve them out. and on the 4th day of December a retreat was ordered to the satisfaction of many. but to the grief of a few brave souls who was among the first that volunteered and who preferred Death in the cause rather than such a disgraceful retreat. We rallied around the brave soul (Colo Milam) and requested him to be our leader, he consented and 150 of us declared to take the place or die in the attempt, while a large number of them endeavored to discourage us and said we would all be butchered, but a few more seen we were resolute and joined untill our number was 220, and on the next morning about day break we marched in the town under heavy fires of their cannon & musketry, but we succeeded in getting possession of some stone houses (which is outside of the square) that sheltered us a little from their fires until we could make Breastworks for ourselves we labored hard day and night for 5 days still gaining possession when on the morning of the 5th day they sent in a flag of truce to the extreme joy of us all, Thus a handful of militia of 220 in number stormed a strongly fotrified place which was supported with two thousand citizens & soldiers (of the enemy) here I must remark, on the third day of the siege our leader fell in battle, another userped the command who never was in favor of storming and had ordered the retreat but he was in time to make a disgraceful treaty, some strongly suspect bribery was the cause but whether or ignorance I cannot decide. The enemy on the third day of the siege raised a black flag (which says no quarters) and when we had whiped them by washing the flag with the blood of about 500 of them we should have made a Treaty and not a childs bargain however its done now and its too late to alter until we have another fight which we expect shortly.

Now a little about myself. I volunteered as a private and as a private in camp was always ready and willing to discharge the duty of a soldier when called on. I was out on a number of scouts and would frequently creep up to the Mexican sentinals at a late hour when they thought alls well and shoot one or two of them a night — and Oh! my dear sister and brothers how often have I thought of you when I have been walking the lonely wood or barren fields as a sentinel exposed to all the inclemencies of the weather and suffering many privations which you can not have the least idea of. but all was sweet when I reflected on our forefathers in the strugle of liberty. about the 28th of October I was appointed 2d Lieut. of artillery and during the siege I was promoted to first on account of the first Lieut. being cashiered for cowardice he always use the word go and I the word come on my brave boys. I thought & still think that nothing but fate save me we only had four killed and thirteen wounded three of the wounded & two of the killed received the shots along side of me when discharging their duty at a cannon that was ordered by a fool in the open street immediately before the enemies breastworks within 120 yards of their heavy fires, but he was my Superior and I did obey and when the men was killed & wounded I loaded and fired the gun assisted by two more instead of ten and escaped only slightly wounded, a ball passed through my hat and cut the flesh to the scull bone and my clothes received many shots until by a lucky shot made by me into the port-hole of the Enemy I dismounted their cannon which caused them to cease firing untill we got ours away — but this is useless to state such trivial sercumstances, the wound never prevented me from working the guns. after we took the place and the child's bargain made, it was thought requisite for some to remain to protect it, volunteers was called for to inlist for four months and did those that came at the eleventh hour and remained in camps expecting us all to be killed and they men of property in this country and have their all in Texas did they come forward to protect the place. No. They pilfered us of our blankets and clothes and horses and went home telling how they whipt the Spaniards reaping the laurels of a few.

Those that fired the first guns at Gonzales and who declared on victory or death. Those who came in when death stared them in the face, and labored hard day and night half starved and almost famished for water, it was them that volunteered to maintain the post untill Texas government could make some provision to keep the Standing army here, and these men have now become almost naked, destitute of funds having expended all for food and munitions of war and not much to eat only some corn that we grind ourselves & poor beef this constitutes our dayly food, but we hourly expect supplies news has arrived that there is plenty of provisions & money and clothes on the way. I hope it's true. I have strayed a little from the subject. when volunteers were called for they were to form into companies and elect their officers-fifty six brave souls joined into a company of artillery and chose me for their Captain. I accepted the command and my dear sister is it possible that the once ignorant weak and fickle minded W. R. Carey should now be at the head of so many brave men as their leader — It is a fact and with his parental name. have I deserved this post of honor, its not for me to say, but the brave proclaimed it, The forces here is commanded by Lieut. Colo J. C. Neill who has his quarters in the Town which is called the left wing of the forces and your brother William has the command of the alamo which is called the right wing I am subject to the orders of Colo Neill but he thinks a great deal of my judgment and consults me about a number of the proceedings before he issues an order. Brothers & sister do not think that I am vain my friends here says I dont possess enough of vanity for my own good, except when we go to fight the Enemy and then I think a small number of us can whip an army of Mexicans — I know one thing, I am deceived in myself.

When I was in Natchitoches I wrote to you and stated I believe that soon I should look out for a companion. It would have happened this winter if the war had not commenced but fortunately it did. My selection was nothing to boast of she is tolerably ugly and tolerably poor and tolerably illiterate. but she is virtuous and a good housekeeper, but there is no prospect now, as I was conversing with a Mexican lady the other day she remarked that in time of peace the ladies would gladly embrace the offer or accept the hand of an officer, but in these war times they would too soon become a widow. She may be right but I dont think it, however, I have too much else to think about now. as I have not been a graduate at West point, I must study military affairs now for I am rejoiced at the opportunity to do something for myself. The men in this place have sometimes been discouraged on account of the distressed situation we are in; for want of clothes and food. The Colo and myself has twice called a general parade and addressed them in such a manner that they would get satisfied for a while, but we are now discouraged ourselves, and unless the provisional government of Texas do speedily send us assistance we will abandon the place, we have sent and made known our situation to them, and as the safety of Texas depends mostly upon the keeping of this place they certainly will as soon as possible do some thing for us especially when we expect to declare independence as soon as the convention meets.

Those of us here has already declared it with a recommendation to the convention of Declaring it but this place is so far in the interior that it takes some time for news to go and supplies to come. The Savage Camancha Indians is near at hand we expect soon to have a fight with them. Since I commenced writing this letter I have received an order to prepare and I have run over it quicker than I would have done as a friend of mine Wm. Guile is going to the States and I thought it a good opportunity as he will put it in the Philadelphia post office and you I think will get it.

I cannot close without saying something about my *invincibles*, as I call them, about twenty of my company (although the whole has been tried and I know them all) that will (to use their words) wade through h-ll, when I am at their head if I should give the order — O sister could you but see me at the head of those brave men marching forward (undismayed) to perform their duty. To relate circumstances of their bravery it would fill a large book. When the enemy ten to one has marched up as if they in one minute would send us all to eternity to see the *invincibles* rush forward charge upon them and put them to flight except those we would either kill or take prisoners. We have had many such scirmishes since we left home, a circumstance occurred the other day which I must relate, a man for disobedience of orders and bad conduct was ordered to arrested (he was not under my command) The officer who received this order took a file of men and attempted to arrest him — he resisted and swore with pistols in his hands that he would shoot down the first man that attempted his arrest, the officer retreated without him the Colo immediately sent an order to me informing me of the circumstance and requesting me to take a file of my *invincibles* and bring the culprit to trial. I ordered three of the brave to prepare immediately I buckled on my sword and went to him he was then with two more who also swore he should not be taken, I approached him with my men he told me if I came one step further he would certainly shoot me down the other two swore the same and with great confidence too as he had put the other off but he soon found himself mistaken my men wanted to rush immediately upon them I ordered them to halt and I walked up to him and with a mild tone told him to disarm himself or I would cut him as-sunder he sheepishly laid down his pistols and gave himself up, the other two swore still that we should not take him. I insignif-icantly look up and told them if they attempted to move or put their finger on the trigger of their arms that they should fall on the spot they stood. I then walked up to them and took their arms likewise, my men stopt where I ordered them, watching minutely their movements ready at the twinkling of an eye to do what I should say, I told them to take those gentlemen to the guardhouse, which was done & there they remained until trial, the court marshall passed a sentence or would have passed a sentence of death upon the first. I found it out and went into my room and wrote two notes one to the court and the other to the Colo. and the sentence was remitted and he was drumed out of the army they all said that nothing but the *invincibles* with Capt Carey could have taken them as he expect-ed to die any way if he was tried. When any thing of a danger-ous character is to be done its by order Capt Carey will take a file from comp. of his men and go immediately and——. its always done. This should not come from me but as I am writ-ing to Brothers and sister I think you ought to know something of these matters — I must close by saying that if I live, as soon as the war is over I will endeavor to see you all. Write to broth-er John or send this letter to him the reason why Brother I dont write to you is I dont know whether you are in Baltimore or not and Brother William & sister I am nearly certain is in the same place yet — Write to me if you please and give as much satisfaction as you can — You will direct to Wm. R. Carey, Washington. Austin's Colony. Texas and I think I will get it, you will have to pay the postage as they will not be taken out of the office in New Orleans unless they are postpaid.

Your affectionate Brother
Wm. R. Carey.[33]

DAVID P. CUMMINGS

Letters Home

Alamo defender David P. Cummings wrote the following letters to his father, David, in Pennsylvania.

Gonzales Texas Jany 20th 1836

Dear Father

The scarcity of paper together with other difficulties I have had to labor under has prevented me from writing before this and indeed it is a matter of Claim whether this letter will ever reach the United States.

I arrived at the mouth of the Brazos about a month ago in a vessel from New Orleans and have traveled on foot by San Felipe to this place leaving my trunk with books, and two rifles with Mr. White at Columbia 10 miles above Brasoria having sold my best rifle for $30 at San Felipe. I saw Genl. Houston and Presented him your letter. He advised me to get a horse & proceed to Goliad where he would see me in a short time *again* — I have accordingly come on thus far with that intention as to connect myself with a Company of Rangers on the Frontiers to keep off the Indians, But it is most probable I will go on to San Antonio de Bexar and there remain until I can suitably connect myself with the Army or until an occasion may require my services. Every man in this country at this time has to go upon his own footing as the Government at present is unable to make any provisions for the Army. However a change for the better is expected soon and affairs is expected to be in a better condition.

Provisions are very scarce here and travelling or living is attended with considerable expense — All owing to the great number of Volunteers from the U. States besides the Emigration of Families into the upper Colonies is unprecedented for the past five months.

Tho under rather indifferent circumstances myself at this time, I have no reason to complain of my coming to this country as I find nothing but what might have been expected. On the contrary I have the satsifaction of beholding one of the finest countries in the world and have fully determined to locate myself in Texas I hope to be better situated to write you more about this country, and as I have not much time Can say very little at present, More than inform you what I am about &c &c.

A Gentleman is going East to day by whom I intend Sending my letter.

Letters have been intercepted to the Mexican citizens of Bexar informing them of the arrival of 2,000 troops on the Rio Grande, and now coming on to retake that place in consequence of which, Many of the Mexicans have secretly left the place, and preparations are now making to fortify the town. All our Troops have been ordered to Copano to proceed against Matamoras.

I remain yours Affectionately
D. P. Cummings[34]

*   *   *

San Antonio de Bexar
February 14th 1836

Dear Father

I wrote you from Gonzales and soon after left ther for this place, yet under different views from what I stated in as a sudden attack was expected on our garrison here and were called on for assistance. It is however fully ascertained that we have nothing of the kind to apprehend before a month or six weeks as the Enemy have not yet crossed the Rio Grande 180 mi. distant from this place nor are they expected to make any movement this way until the weather becomes warm or until the grass is sufficiently up to support their horses we conceive it however important to be prepared as a heavy attack is expected from Sant Ana himself in the Spring as no doubt the despot will use every possible means and strain every nerve to conquer and exterminate us from the land — in this we have no fear and are confident that Texas cannot only sustain what she now holds but take Mexico itself did She think on conquest.

The northern Indians have joined to our assistance and the volunteers from the United States are every day flocking to our ranks which from the liberal promises of the Government and desirable resources of the Country seem determined to sustain themselves or sinke in the attempt. Many it is true have left the country and returned home to their friends and pleasures byt of such Texas has no use for and her agents in the U. States should be careful whom they send us for assistance we want men of determined spirits, that can undergo hardships and deprivation Otherwise they are only a pest and expense to their fellow Soldiers— to the first class (tho I would be the last to advise in any case), I say come on, there is a fine field open to you all no matter how you are situated or what may be your circumstances. At least come and see the country, as a farmer, mechanic or a Soldier you will do well — I believe no country offers such strong inducements to Emmigration, affording all the conviences of life that man can devise — what I write is from my own observation and from what I hear from those who have resided for years in the Country. I am to leave this to return to the Cibilo Creek in company with 10 others to take up, our lands we get as citizens which in more then 1100 acres for single men, men of family 4428 acres our our volunteer pay is 20$ per month & 640 acres at close of war.

Any communication to San Felipe de Austin you may make with postage paid to the Boundary line I will get or send to Stiles Duncan Natchitoches, he could mail it to San Felipe as I would be very glad to hear from you all.

It might be that I might be of some benefit to you here provided any of you could have a mind to come out and indeed to speak sincearly this would be the Country for us all, nothing could induce me from my determination of settling here, tho my disposition may not be like most others. I should like you could once see it. — a visit by Jonathan would improve his health I have been very healthy since I have been here and am improving.

Yours affectionately,
D. P. Cummings

P.S.

There is one thing might be proper for me to add members have been elected to a convention of all Texas to meet on 1st March, which will make an immediate declaration of independence — upon the faith of this event great speculation is going on in Lands, tho the office for the disposal of the public lands is not yet opened but is expected will be in a Short time. The price of Land has risen greatly since the commencement of the war, and a declaration of Independence will bring them to vie with those of the U. States tho — they can be purchased from 50 cts to 5$ per acre by the League depending as their improvement. Or convenience to settlements — not Country is now settling faster — As I will most likely be engaged in surveying of public lands I might be of service to some of our friends in procurring disirable or choice locations.

D. P. Cummings[35]

JOHN HARRIS

Crockett's Cousin

Virginia Bronson presented the oral evidence for the following story. Bronson is a great-great-great-great-granddaughter of Siden B. Harris, who, according to family legend, was an uncle to Alamo defender John Harris. Documentation has never been found to support the family legend.

David Crockett spoke enthusiastically of a great journey to Texas, and when he did, John Harris listened. A new beginning in a new land sounded like a good idea to Harris. So Harris gladly followed his famous cousin for the Mexican province.

Land was what Harris and Crockett sought, and they leisurely prospected potential settlements along with their traveling companions.

In time, they learned of the 640-acre bounty of land given to each soldier who took up arms for Texas independence. Harris and Crockett were game. They would become part of the group popularly known as the "Tennessee Mounted Volunteers," and they would die side by side March 6, 1836, at the Alamo.[36]

Sketch of David Crockett telling stories to boys in Bastrop County.
— Drawing by Gary Zaboly

GEORGE WASHINGTON COTTLE

Shadow of the Alamo

Billie Matthews and Ralph Love presented the oral evidence for the following story. Matthews is a great-great-great-niece to Alamo defender George Washington Cottle and a great-great-granddaughter of Texan Zebulon Pike Cottle. Love is George Washington Cottle's great-great-great-nephew and Zebulon Pike Cottle's great-great-grandson.

Zebulon Pike Cottle never forgot the Alamo. His uncle "Wash" died within its walls.

Cottle's uncle, George Washington Cottle, rode into the Alamo with thirty-one other volunteers from Gonzales in March of 1836. The news of his uncle's death came to Zebulon months later.

The story told to Zebulon and other family members was of George vowing to never let the Mexican soldiers get their hands on the garrison's ammunition supply. He was said to have been found dead in the magazine room of the Alamo chapel.[37]

Two months earlier, eleven-year-old Zebulon and another boy were playing on a road in what is today Bastrop County. A man rode up, hopped down off his horse, and sat down on a rock to rest.

The man whittled on a piece of wood as he told the boys stories. With each tale, the boys became more interested. Finally, the man stood up and told the boys he had to leave. The boys asked him where he was going.

"I'm Davy Crockett," the man said with a smile. "I'm on my way to the Alamo."[38]

Sketch of William Wells, Sr., sleeping in the gut of a tree and being found by Crockett.

— Drawing by Gary Zaboly

WILLIAM WELLS, SR.

Gone to Texas

Oral evidence for the following story was presented by Dodie and William Austin Pugh, Jr. William is a great-great-great-grandson of Alamo defender William Wells, Sr.

William Wells, Jr., had given up hope of ever again seeing his father, William Wells, Sr. His father had packed up and left one day years before when he was younger, and was never heard from again by anyone in the family.

Some said he became despondent over the death of his second wife, Nancy Kelton, and ran away.[39] But where did he go? Was he still alive? There were never any letters or telegrams to fill in the blanks. Memories were all that remained.

All that changed one day when an attorney came to William Wells, Jr., in 1854.

The man told the younger Wells he was being sought by the Republic of Texas for a bounty of land which was owed to him for the military service of his deceased father. Wells, Jr., listened closely as the man unraveled a family mystery with each new sentence.

William Wells, Sr., died in defense of the Alamo March 6, 1836, in Bexar. He died a hero, alongside American legends such as David Crockett and James Bowie.[40]

Answers to one mystery about his father, however, only led to more questions. Why did he go to Texas? Did he travel alone? And how did he end up at the Alamo? The son would spend the remainder of his days piecing together his father's final journey.

William Wells, Jr., and his family would discover that Wells, Sr., went into Tennessee from his home in Hall County, Georgia. From Tennessee, where it was rumored he again married, he then traveled down through Arkansas and into Texas.

One night en route to Texas, Wells, Sr., stopped to set up camp. He was found sleeping in the hollow of a large tree when a band of fellow Americans rode up. Crockett, the famed frontiersman, was the leader of the group who discovered the sleepy traveler.[41]

Crockett and the others asked to join William at his campsite for the night, and he was more than happy to have the company.

In the morning, Crockett asked William if he wanted to join them in the fight for Texas independence. William took Crockett up on his offer. He figured he had nothing better to do.[42]

DAVID CROCKETT

Faithful to the End

Frances Kerr John presented the oral evidence for the following passage. John is a great-great-great-granddaughter of David Crockett. The first letter in this passage was written to Crockett's widow, Elizabeth, on August 12, 1836, by Isaac N. Jones, who encountered the celebrated frontiersman on his journey into Texas. The second letter was written by David to his daughter on January 9, 1836, from San Augustine, Texas.

Elizabeth Crockett opened the thick, heavy envelope and pulled out its contents. A letter was accompanied by a watch, which she instantly recognized. The watch belonged to her husband, the famous David Crockett, whom she was told died five months earlier in Texas at a small mission fortress called the Alamo.[43]

She began to read.

Lost Prairie, Arkansas, 1836

Mrs. David Crockett

Dear Madam:

Permit me to introduce myself to you as one of the acquaintances of your much respected husband, Colonel Crockett. With his fate in the Fortress San Antonio, Texas, you are doubtless long since advised. With such feelings of sympathy, I regret his untimely loss to your family and self. For if amongst

Portrait of David Crockett from Smithsonian Institution.

strangers he constituted the most agreeable companion, he doubtless to his beloved wife and children must have been a favorite peculiarly prized. In his loss Freedom has been deprived of one of her bravest sons in whose bosom universal philanthropy glowed with as genial warmth as ever animated the heart of an American citizen. When he fell, a soldier died. To bemoan his fate is to pay a tribute of grateful respect to Nature — he seemed to be her son.

The object of this letter is to beg that you will accept the watch which accompanies it. You will doubtless know it when you see it and, as it has his name engraved on its surface, it will no doubt be the more acceptable to you.

As it will probably be gratifying to you to learn in what way I become possessed of it, permit me to state that last winter (the precise date not recollected by me) Col. Crockett, in company with several other gentlemen, passed through Lost Prairie on Red River (where I live). The company preceding the Colonel who was a little behind rode up to my house and asked for accommodations for the night. My family being so situated from the indisposition of my wife that I could not accomodate them, they got quarters at one of my neighbor's houses. The Colonel visited me the next day and spent the day with me. He observed while here that his funds were getting short and as a means of recruiting them he must sell something. He proposed to me to exchange watches. He priced his watch at thirty dollars more than mine, which sum I paid him and we accordingly exchanged.

With his open frankness, his natural honesty of expression, his perfect want of concealment, I could not but be very much pleased. And with a hope that it might be an accommodation to him, I was gratified at the exchange as it gave me a keepsake which would often remind me of an honest man, a good citizen, and a pioneer in the cause of liberty amongst his suffering brethren in Texas.

His military career was short. Though I deeply lament his death, I cannot restrain my American smile at the recollection of the fact that he died as a United States soldier should die; covered with the slain enemy and even in death presenting to them in his clenched hands the weapons of their destruction.

We hope that the day is not far distant when his adopted country will be freed from savage enemy and afford to yourself and children a home rendered in every way comfortable by the liberal donations of her government.

Accept, dear madam, for yourself and family the most sincere wishes for your future happiness of.

Your most obedient servant & friend,
Isaac N. Jones[44]

Elizabeth wiped the tears from her eyes. A flood of emotions overwhelmed her yet again. For the past five months, she heard conflicting reports. Did Davy die? Was he massacred at the Alamo by the Mexicans? Or was he taken prisoner? Maybe he escaped. She prayed.

The scenarios — both tragic and promising — rushed through her head. Still, she refused to believe the stories of his death.

Years earlier, Davy set out one December morning on a six-mile trek through the thick wilderness of western Tennessee to fetch a keg of gunpowder from his brother-in-law's cabin. Hypothermia set in as a result of the grueling wet, cold journey, and he was forced to delay his return home until the weather improved. This prompted his distressed wife to dispatch a hand to search for him.

Davy, determined to return to his family "or die a-trying," finally decided to brave the snowy wilderness. Elizabeth's worst fears vanished when Davy appeared at their cabin door with the keg of gunpowder and even freshly hunted meat.[45]

So why should this episode in Texas be any different? The last time the family heard from Davy he sounded happy and safe. She recalled his last letter, written to his daughter:

San Augustine, Texas
January 9, 1836

My dear Son and Daughter: this is the first time I have had the opportunity to write to you with convenience. I am now blessed with excellent health, and am in high spirits, although I have had many difficulties to encounter. I have got through safe and have been received by everybody with open arms of friendship, I am hailed with a hearty welcome to this country, a dinner and a party of Ladys have honored me with an invitation to participate with them, both in Nacogdoches and this place; the cannon was fired here on my arrival and I must say as to What I have seen of Texas, it is the garden spot of the world, the best land & best prospects for health I ever saw is here, and I do believe it is a fortune to any man to come here; there is a world of country to settle, it is not required to pay down for your league of land; every man is entitled to his head-right of 4438 A. and they may make the money to pay for it off the land.

I expect in all probability to settle on the Bodark or Chocktaw Bayou of Red River, that I have no doubt is the richest country in the world, good land, plenty of timber, and the best springs, and good mill streams, good range, clear water & every appearance of health – game a plenty. It is in the pass where the buffalo passes from the north to south and back twice a year and bees and honey a plenty.

I have a great hope of getting the agency to settle that country and I would be glad to see every friend I have settle there, it would be a fortune to them all. I have taken the oath of the government and have enrolled my name as a volunteer for six months, and will set out for the Rio Grande in a few days with the volunteers of the U.S., but all volunteers are entitled to a vote for a member of the convention and these members are to be voted for; and I have but little doubt of being elected a member to form the Constitution for the Provence. I am rejoiced at my fate. I had rather be in my present situation than to be elected to a seat in Congress for life. I am in great hopes of making a fortune for myself and family bad as has been my prospects. I have not wrote to William but have requested John to direct him what to do. I hope you show him this letter and also your brother John as it is not convenient at this time for me to write them. I hope you will do the best you can and I will do the same, do not be uneasy about me I am with my friends. I must close with great respects

Your affectionate father, Farewell

David Crockett[46]

Even after receiving the letter from Isaac Jones, Elizabeth vowed to never give up hope of Davy returning home. Yet this time did feel different.

A dreadful premonition had hit her the day Davy donned his fox-skinned hat and buckskins and headed for Texas. As she waved goodbye to him with one hand and shaded her eyes with the other, she felt sick inside. Elizabeth made it known to Davy she didn't want him to go.

Suddenly, he vanished into the woods and was gone.

The family was silent and then Elizabeth said solemnly, "I don't feel like I'll ever see him again."[47]

And she never did.

Years later, after the family had relocated to Texas on the bounty of land given for Davy's military service, Elizabeth still held out hope of his return. Each morning she would walk out on the front porch of her house, shade her eyes, and look off into the horizon.

Maybe, just maybe, she thought, Davy would someday come walking back into her life.

On the morning of January 31, 1860, Elizabeth again made her daily trip to the front porch, looking off in the distance. Davy was nowhere to be found. Elizabeth collapsed on the porch and died of a stroke.[48]

JOHN McGREGOR

Listen to the Wind

Tylene Edminston presented oral evidence for the following legend. Edminston has collected various legends on the McGregor clan, and according to her family tales, Alamo defender John McGregor had a brother. Edminston descends from that brother, and if true, she would be a distant niece of the Alamo's famed Scotsman. Documentation has never been found to support this claim.

Red-head John McGregor wailed away on his bagpipes while those around him in the Nacogdoches tavern whooped it up and laughed. Rowdy frontiersmen, local farmers, and general travelers had congregated at the pub to have a good time and, perhaps, to forget the troubles of the day.

Texas was knee-deep in a revolution for independence from Mexico. Everyone felt the tension mounting, so there was no time like the present to blow off steam.

McGregor's therapy was his bagpipes, which he had learned to play in his native Scotland. No one in the tavern, however, knew if McGregor was any good or not. They just clapped their hands and stomped their feet to the strange music.

The cheers became exceptionally loud when a man who entered the tavern was introduced as the famous frontiersman David Crockett. The buckskin pioneer was accompanied by a small entourage of men, and there were plenty of handshakes and slaps on the back as he made his way across the room. McGregor promptly struck up another tune much to the delight of the tavern's notable guest.

Once McGregor completed his song, Crockett climbed on a wooden crate and addressed those in the tavern. Amiable Crockett turned serious for a moment. Mexico was looking for a fight, Crockett told the crowd, because Texans were becoming too free. If Mexico was looking for a fight, he continued as the crowd listened intently, then he would give it to them. He said he and his men were going wherever Texas needed help. Their next stop would be a place called the Alamo in San Antonio de Bexar.

Crockett concluded by asking, "Who will join me?"

McGregor tugged on his red beard as the crowd roared with approval. He owned more than 4,000 acres of cattle land in Nacogdoches, and there was no way he was going to be pushed off his land by some dictator. He had moved to Texas to be free. His people had left Scotland because they refused to change their name and live in fear.

John McGregor. He liked the ring. His name was a badge of honor. Besides, he thought, had there ever been a McGregor who didn't like a good fight?

McGregor called out to Crockett, "I'll fight."

Crockett took an instant liking to his new recruits from Nacogdoches, especially McGregor. He and McGregor were both free spirits who loved a good fight as well as good music. Crockett played the fiddle, and in his own right was an accomplished musician.

Yet danger lurked ahead, and it didn't take long for them to come to that realization. Crockett's party spent much of its travel time to Bexar dodging Mexican scouts. Finally, after a hectic journey, they arrived safely at the Alamo, an old Spanish mission turned fortress.

Crockett, McGregor and the rest of the "Tennessee Boys," including Micajah Autry and Daniel Cloud, were immediately welcomed.

Fellow adventurer James Bowie warmly greeted Crockett and his hardy men. Crockett and McGregor soon learned Bowie, a famed knife fighter, was also a natural born leader. They saw Bowie on several occasions command with authority, rally the troops, and boost the spirits of the men in the garrison single-handedly.

When Bowie became gravely ill, confined to one of the rooms in the low barracks, Texas had big boots to fill. Bowie's absence greatly damaged the spirits of the men, some of whom deserted in large numbers and others who turned to liquor.

Crockett used his wits to take charge. He grabbed his fiddle and challenged McGregor to a musical duel with his bagpipes. The idea was to keep the defenders occupied and their spirits high. Every time there was a lull in the fighting, Crockett and McGregor matched their talents on their musical instruments.

The ploy worked. Morale soared to new heights. At night around the several compound campfires, Crockett and McGregor would entertain their comrades with music. There was always a challenge to play better and louder. Men huddled around the campfires for fear of getting their throats slashed in the dark of the night. But there was always the music of Crockett and McGregor to comfort them.

Crockett and McGregor thus played every day and every night.

In the early morning hours of March 6, one could hear Crockett's fiddle and McGregor's bagpipes as the Mexicans scaled the walls. The music echoed as the hand-to-hand combat became fierce.

One of Lieutenant Colonel Travis' final orders was to blow up the powder room should the Alamo fall. Travis did not want the powder in enemy hands. So, in the waning minutes of the battle, with death surely imminent, Crockett grabbed a torch and dashed for the powder room. Crockett was cut down by the Mexican soldiers, and McGregor picked up the torch to finish his friend's mission.

The brave Scotsman met the same fate as Crockett, how-

Portrait of James Bowie.

— By George P. A. Healy

ever, and the torch was then scooped up by defender Gregorio Esparza. He, too, was killed before reaching the magazine room.

But the music never stopped.

Some say if you visit the Alamo today, and listen to the wind, you can still hear Crockett playing the fiddle and McGregor playing the bagpipes.[49]

MARCUS L. SEWELL

ANDREW JACKSON SOWELL

Fate

The following story is based on a June 23, 1981, letter from R. L. Sowell to a Mr. Long. Sowell is a great-great-great-nephew of Andrew Jackson Sowell, who was sent from the Alamo to obtain provisions.

Poor Marcus L. Sewell, his cousins always said with pity. Plain and simple.

Sewell, a cousin of Texas pioneer John Newton Sowell, was fresh off the boat from England when he got tangled in the Texan war for indepedence. The feisty Englishman was a recent arrival to Texas when he volunteered to ride with the Gonzales Ranging Company of Mounted Volunteers.

Sewell and thirty-one other brave men in the company rode to the aid of the men in the Alamo and never lived to tell their story. Sewell instead crossed into the halls of Texas heroes when he perished March 6, 1836, along with the rest of the defiant garrison to the overwhelming forces of the Mexican Army.

Fate certainly can be quirky.

The Sowells always added the story of how Sewell — the cousin who spelled his name funny — ended up in the Alamo. Cousin Andrew Jackson Sowell was one of the men who recruited Sewell.

Sowell and his friend Byrd Lockhart were already in the Alamo when Lieutenant Colonel Travis sent them to secure supplies and reinforcements. They knew the countryside as well as anyone in the compound at the time, so they were the natural choice to ride out.

Lockhart and Sowell were delayed in Gonzales, however, trying to purchase cattle and supplies. Farmers in the region were reluctant to sell or give away any cattle or oxen. So the two men waited and waited in hopes some farmers would change their minds.

The delay saved Sowell's life. The Alamo fell before he could return. But the cousin he recruited, Marcus Sewell, would not be so lucky.

Such is fate.[50]

ANTHONY WOLF

Black Sheep

Regina Pierce presented the oral evidence for the following story. Pierce is a great-great-niece of Alamo defender Anthony Wolf. She heard stories about her famed ancestor from her uncle, Dave Wolf.

Opportunities were boundless in the Mexican province of Texas for pirate Jean Lafitte and his followers from New Orleans. Free from the watchful eye of the United States government, they could raid passing ships under a Mexican flag and re-establish their dominance in that coastal region.

Mexico was busy with a brewing revolution, thus leaving Lafitte and his motley crew of Baratarians to reign as they desired. So in 1817, a small fleet and a few of Lafitte's former men moved their operation to Galveston.[51] Anthony Wolf was one of those men.[52]

Wolf had run with Lafitte in New Orleans. He was one of many to follow the famous buccaneer to Texas, where they smuggled booty and slaves back across the American border into Louisiana. Lafitte also sold slaves to Texas immigrants.

Lafitte's force was 1,000 strong before long.

The Galveston settlement offered a strange mix. Many of Lafitte's pirates brought along women — African-Americans, Native Americans, and a few white women. Some of the women were prostitutes from New Orleans.[53]

Lafitte's stronghold in Galveston lasted until his departure in either 1820 or 1821.[54] But in his wake he left a band of pirates, including Wolf. Their next great adventure would come in the spring of 1836.

When word of the Alamo's call for help against the onrushing Mexican Army reached Galveston, Wolf and other scalawags quickly responded. The hardy gang of pirates rode all-out to aid those entrapped at the Bexar mission.

Wolf was killed along with other Alamo defenders on March 6, 1836. Their bodies were unceremoniously piled on wood and burned.

Since Wolf was the black sheep of the family, his relatives didn't talk much about him. Alamo survivor Susanna Dickinson did remember a man named "Wollf" in an 1878 interview with journalist Charles W. Evers of Ohio. Evers wrote, "She says that only one man, named Wolff, asked for quarter, but was instantly killed. The wretched man had two little boys, aged 11 and 12 years. The little fellows came to Mrs. Dickerson's (Dickinson's) room, where Mexicans killed them and a man named Walker, and carried the boys bodies out on their bayonets."[55]

Was this Lafitte's pirate?

PART II

Inside the Walls

From the moment the Alamo fell, people have tried to piece together the garrison's final hours.

Rumors of the Alamo's fate swept across the prairie with surprising swiftness in 1836, but details were almost always sketchy and hard to confirm. Frontier communication was often reduced to word-of-mouth.

Perhaps nowhere in Texas was the need to know the Alamo's fate more powerful than at the Independence Convention at Washington-on-the-Brazos. While members of the Convention hashed out a constitution for the fledgling republic, tension mounted over the lack of news from Bexar.

William Fairfax Gray, an astute Virginian, probably summed up the feelings of those in attendance when he penned in his diary:

> No news yet from the Alamo, and much anxiety is felt for the fate of the brave men there. It is obvious that they must be surrounded and all communication with them cut off.[1]

Gray wrote those words on March 10. Three days later, Gray again made a notation in his diary concerning the Alamo:

> No intelligence yet from the Alamo. The anxiety begins to be intense. Mr. Badgett and Dr. Goodrich, members of the Convention, have brothers there, and Mr. Grimes, another member, has a son there.[2]

Citizens in Gonzales anxiously awaited news from the Alamo. Thirty-two of the town's men rode to the aid of the troops there, but days had passed without any word or the sound of cannon. A town was on edge.

First details of the battle were told to residents of Gonzales by two *vaqueros* from Bexar, Anselmo Borgara and Andres Barcena. They said the Alamo was overrun and slaughtered to a man.

On March 11 General Houston arrived in Gonzales to find the townspeople in a panic. He promptly moved to defuse the situation and tossed the two *vaqueros* in jail as spies.[3]

Survivor Susanna Dickinson would confirm the Alamo's defeat the next day with a firsthand report.

On March 20, 1836, members of the Convention received their first account of the Mexicans' victory at the Alamo from Joe, a slave of Lieutenant Colonel Travis.

Joe provided a rare glimpse of what actually took place inside the Alamo's walls while being "interrogated in the presence of the cabinet and others." He told of Travis thrusting a sword into a Mexican officer as he took his last breath of life . . . of James Bowie firing a gun from his sick bed . . . of David Crockett and his friends being found with twenty-four dead Mexicans around them.[4]

In Mexico, word of the battle reached the interior via a courier who was sent from the Alamo March 7. He delivered a letter written by an unidentified Mexican *soldado*, who gave his own fascinating insights. The *soldado* wrote:

> We carried ladders, beams, bars, pich-axes etc.: although the distance was short, we suffered to be able to get through the canister shot of two guns that shot down more than forty men: the tenacious resistance of our enemy was to be admired and the dauntless constancy of all the generals, officers and troops: it seemed as though the cannon balls and bullets from the muskets and rifles of the enemy were dulled by the chests of our soldiers, who ceaselessly were shouting *Long live the Mexican Republic! Long live General Santa Anna!*. . . .
>
> The four columns and the reserves as if by magic scaled all at once, the enemy walls and threw themselves inside after about three quarters of an hour under horrible fire, which once stopped, a horrible battle ensued at sword point; and afterwards, a pitiful but unavoidable massacre of the ungrateful colonists took place. . . . Their chief named Trawis [Travis] died

a brave man with his gun in hand, behind a cannon, but the perverse and braggart Santiago Bowie [James Bowie], died like a woman, hidden almost under a mattress. . . .[5]

In the years that followed, other details of the battle would surface from various sources.

Dr. John Sutherland, who left the Alamo as a courier, visited the compound two years after the battle. He claimed to have seen the blood stains on the walls where Bowie's brains were spattered.[6]

Mexican officer Jose Enrique de la Pena recounted a story in his diary of a defender who leaped from one of the garrison's highest points with a boy in his arms. The two were killed on impact.[7]

Relatives of Alamo defenders called on Susanna Dickinson on several ocassions. They always hoped to learn some precious information about the last hours of their loved ones. A number of family legends were created out of these visits.

Dickinson's tesimony would also be used for various newspaper interviews, as well as by the Republic of Texas to verify the presence of numerous defenders. Enrique Esparza, another Alamo survivor, would also go public with his story. Unfortunately, their accounts often conflict with those of other eyewitnesses.

Still, with each new story, the legend grew. No one could get enough information about the famous last stand.

One hundred and sixty years later, the fascination continues.

People yearn to know more about what unfolded in the days leading up to the Alamo's last hour. Numerous archaeological digs have been undertaken since 1836. Since 1966 alone, approximately eleven such digs have been conducted, all in hopes of unearthing more clues.

How did Davy really die? What kind of illness did Bowie have? And did Travis really believe help was on the way? Descendants, historians, and other interested parties are still trying to piece together the story.

The cold fact, says Alamo Battlefield Association President Kevin R. Young, is this: "There are things we'll never really know for sure."[8]

Nonetheless, the hunt continues. Every piece of evidence is priceless.

William Barret Travis

WILLIAM BARRET TRAVIS

Victory or Death

Alamo commander William Barret Travis seemed to define the struggle for Texas independence more than any other man of his time. Here are two of his famed letters which Texans have cherished for generations.

Feb. 24, 1836

To the People of Texas & all Americans in the world —

Fellow citizens and Compatriots – I am besieged by a thousand or more of the Mexicans under Santa Anna. I have sustained a continual Bombardment & cannonade for 24 hours & have not lost a man. The enemy has demanded a surrender at discretion, otherwise, the garrison are to be put to the sword, if the fort is taken. I have answered the demand with a cannon shot, & our flag still waves proudly from the walls. I shall never surrender or retreat. Then, I call on you in the name of Liberty, of patriotism & everything dear to the American character to come to our aid with all dispatch. The enemy is receiving reinforcements daily & will no doubt increase to three or four thousand in four or five days. If this call is neglected, I am determined to sustain myself as long as possible & die like a soldier who never forgets what is due his own honor & that of his country. *VICTORY or DEATH.*

William Barret Travis

P.S. The Lord is on our side. When the enemy appeared in sight we had not three bushels of corn. We have since found in deserted houses 80 to 90 bushels and got into the walls 20 or 30 head of Beeves.[9]

Those immortal words have long since gone down in Texas history. What may be even more endearing to Texans, however, are the words Travis scribbled on a torn, soiled piece of wrapping paper three days before the final assault.

The note was addressed to David Ayers, who lived near Washington-on-the-Brazos. Ayers was taking care of the lieutentant colonel's son, Charles Edward, whom Travis obviously thought about often in his final hours.

In a hurry, Travis scrawled these words:

> Take care of my little boy. If the country should be saved, I may make him a splendid fortune; but if the country should be lost and I should perish, he will have nothing but the proud recollection that he is the son of a man who died for his country.[10]

BLAS HERRERA

Warning

Adolph Herrera presented the oral evidence for the following story. Herrera is a great-great-grandson of Blas Herrera, who was an Alamo scout and courier.

Blas Herrera and his fellow Native American scouts watched as the Mexican Army poured across the Rio Grande. They remained hidden in some distant brush as they watched one company after another cross.

The numbers were staggering.

Herrera knew he was watching the main body of the Mexican Army led by General Santa Anna, and he needed to report back to Juan Seguin in Bexar as soon as possible. Seguin, who led a band of local *Tejanos* in Bexar, sent Herrera to Laredo in hopes he could gain some intelligence on the advancing Mexican Army.

Herrera saw more than he wanted. Mexican companies were coming from all over, and he was staring at by far the largest force.

Seguin sent Herrera on this mission because he was his best fighter and most experienced scout. Herrera lived up to this reputation on the nights that followed.

Each night when the sun set and the Mexicans bedded down for sleep, Herrera and his Native American companions became assassins. They pounced on Mexican sentries in the stillness of the night and slashed their throats. A great number of Mexican soldiers were killed by Herrera's gang, which always managed to disappear into the darkness untouched and unseen.

Santa Anna's army was constantly sabotaged by Herrera's gang en route to Bexar. Bridges were destroyed in hopes of slowing Santa Anna's progress, and Native Americans were left behind to harass the unwelcome army every step of the way.

Herrera eventually parted with his loyal companions to carry the news to Seguin. The brave *Tejano* leader waited for Herrera in a crumbling adobe mission called the Alamo just outside of Bexar. Roughly 200 Texians, including some of Seguin's men, were working to strengthen the Alamo against a Mexican attack when Herrera rode up. Herrera reported directly to Seguin.

More than 1,000 Mexicans had crossed the Rio Grande. Herrera looked around the Alamo compound.

"To stay here," he said, "would be suicide."

Seguin had Herrera repeat his findings to the Alamo commanders — Lt. Col. William Barret Travis, Col. James Bowie, and Col. David Crockett among others. They listened to Herrera's claims with suspicion.

Finally, one of the Texans interrupted Herrera.

"Crazy Mexican," he said. "You're drunk."

Shocked and insulted, Herrera stormed off. Seguin followed.

A heated debate soon erupted. Not everyone who listened to Herrera's report thought he was crazy. More than 1,000 Mexican soldiers were indeed marching toward Bexar. What should be done next?

General Houston's orders were to burn down the Alamo and Bexar. Bowie was outraged at this suggestion and took his concerns to Seguin, who shared Bowie's disdain for such an absurd plan.

Native families should be considered, Seguin argued. Burning Bexar was not an option, he finally said in anger, and he immediately dispatched Herrera to deliver this message to Houston.

Seguin's protest was honored by Houston.

The Texas general kept Herrera in the process. He wanted the experienced *Tejano* scout by his side at all times, and this move paid off one month later at the Battle of San Jacinto. Herrera was one of the scouts who insisted on surprising the Mexican soldiers while most of them slept on April 21.

Herrera knew the Mexican Army's every move — when it partied, when it rested, and when it marched. Herrera also knew when to attack.

Houston obliged, listening to Herrera's tips, and Texas was saved. The Mexican Army was soundly routed.

Those at the Alamo weren't as fortunate. They had not listened to Herrera. A brutal death was their fate. Santa Anna's army of 1,500 swarmed and overwhelmed the Texians on the morning of March 6.

Native Americans, recruited in the mountains of Mexico en route to Texas by Santa Anna, led the vicious attack. The Indians did most of the damage wielding machetes, each cutting down several defenders within minutes.

From his home in Bexar, *Alcalde* Jose Francisco Ruiz listened to the booming cannonade which shook the walls around him. Ruiz, Herrera's father-in-law, was placed under house arrest by Santa Anna.

Ruiz didn't flee Bexar because he knew Santa Anna would not harm the native people, only those who rebelled. He was right.

In twenty-five minutes, the gunfire began to subside. The battle was over.

Ruiz was led from his home along with other *Tejanos* in Bexar and ordered to gather the dead. The Alamo slain were piled on layers of wood, roughly 200 in all. Some 500 Mexicans who perished in the fight were buried at various locations around Bexar.

Someone suggested dumping some of the bodies into the river, but Ruiz scoffed at the idea. He firmly refused to dump the dead into the town's drinking water.

When the morbid task was done, and the survivors were taken into town for questioning, Ruiz watched the Mexicans set fire to the Alamo dead.

Clouds of black smoke rose from the raging flames. A ghastly glow soon lit up the sky.

Ruiz watched the gigantic bonfire as he shook his head in disgust.

The slaughter could have been avoided, he thought, if only the defenders had not been so stubborn. Yet he knew their motives for staying varied from man to man. Some were spies for the American government, he believed, while others were arrogant bullies. Still others were just simple farmers. Their lives could have been saved had they only listened to Herrera's warning.

These men died a heroic death, Ruiz thought, but they were fools.[11]

JUAN N. SEGUIN

Heroic Tejano

Oral evidence for the following legend was presented by Albert Seguin-Carvajal Gonzales, a great-great-great-grandson of Alamo courier Juan N. Seguin. Gonzales heard stories of Seguin from his grandmother, Maria Lucrecia Seguin-Carvajal Ramirez.

Texas has never had a shortage of heroes, and none have been any bigger than *Tejano* Juan Seguin and David Crockett. Perhaps it was only fitting these two Texas giants developed a special friendship during the war for independence.

Seguin, a renowned *Tejano*, first met the famed Tennessee frontiersman within the walls of the Alamo in 1836. Both men had been thrown together by the spirit of an independence movement known as the Texas Revolution.

Freedom, both men agreed, was worth dying for.

Crockett's notoriety was well established by the time he first shook hands with Seguin. A former congressman, a famed naturalist, and the best rifle shot in Tennessee, Crockett's reputation was well known to Seguin.

Likewise, Crockett was very familiar with Seguin's tall stature among the Texas people. Crockett had heard several stories of Seguin's beautiful horses, and his spacious ranch, and it didn't take long before he was informed of Seguin's keen marksmanship.

Seguin and Crockett were drawn together by common interest. Naturally, a friendship quickly developed.

The two talked at length about farming, ranching, and hunting. They were especially captivated by hunting, which was not just a sport, but a way of life. Hunting was the means by which each provided food for his family.

Cultural barriers hardly slowed down Seguin and Crockett. They agreed on many subjects, including the powderkeg of politics in Texas.

Crockett told Seguin that what he and the other *Tejanos* were going through with the war was similar to what the United States had gone through during its fight for independence. Brothers fighting brothers. Englishmen fighting English colonists. Everything was the same.

Crockett's unique way of speaking impressed Seguin, but his words weren't those he wanted to hear. Seguin said war was a subject he didn't want to think about, and that any blood spilled was a "waste of God's creations" — Texian or Mexican.

Seguin's roots ran deep into Texas, and no matter how hard he tried, he could never remove the pain he felt over the brewing trouble in his land. After all, he was part of Texas, like the rivers, the valleys, or the Comanches.

For it was Seguin's father, Erasmo, who opened the door to *Tejas* for Stephen F. Austin to bring American settlers in to colonize the territory. Even then, Erasmo believed *Tejas* would eventually become an indepenent country. It was only a matter of time.

Don Erasmo based his belief on the constant turmoil in Mexico. First there was Mexico's fight for independence from Spain and then the current government regime headed by the dictator Santa Anna.

Never did he believe in those early years, however, that his family would be part of the history-making equation.

Juan Seguin had his own theories. He first became suspicious of the new government following its break with Spain. One day, possibly one day soon, he thought, he would have to take a stand. He knew the decisions would not be easy, but they would ultimately set the course for his family's future and that of his country.

That moment of truth came sooner than he thought. Where would Seguin's allegiance ultimately rest? The decision gnawed at his heart.

Seguin never thought of the Anglo as an intruder into his country. Neither did his father. All people had always been welcomed at his father's ranch, Casa Blanca. But not every *Tejano* agreed with Seguin, who cared for all people. Thus, Crockett's words — "Brothers fighting brothers" — echoed painfully in his mind.

Realizing he struck the wrong nerve with his new friend, Crockett gracefully changed the subject.

He quickly shifted the conversation to marksmanship, which he knew was sure to set off a friendly debate. He was right.

* * *

Seguin and some of his loyal *vaqueros* were busy training the new recruits how to ride horses like Mexicans so they would be on equal terms with the professionally schooled Mexican cavalry.

Crockett called out to Seguin and jokingly told him he was wasting his time training men to ride and shoot at the same time. The Mexican *soldados*, Crockett hollered, will all be on foot.

Seguin politely corrected his friend, noting the number of Mexican cavalrymen would be much larger than those of the foot *soldados*.

"Well," Crockett replied, "how in tar nation do you know that?"

"Mexican men in Mexico are generally shorter than the Mexican *Tejano*," Seguin explained. "So they put the shorter men on horseback and the long-legged men on foot so as to keep a steady march."

Laughter erupted from the walls of the Alamo.

"Hey, Seguin," Crockett shouted, "you've been out in the sun too long. You're beginning to sound like you're from Tennessee."

"I think that was a compliment, but in case it wasn't, the truth of the matter is I'm not teaching these men to ride. I'm teaching these beautiful mustangs. They will be turned loose tomorrow in the path of the oncoming Mexican Army. They will gallop up to the Alamo and abruptly stop within a hundred paces, just long enough for you to be able to get off a good shot."

Laughter again broke out from Crockett and others listening. Crockett's voice then became stern.

"Look here, Seguin," Crockett said, "I'm glad that you brought up the subject of shooting. I do believe we should put all curiosities aside by having ourselves a good ol' turkey shoot. So as soon as this little conflict is over, all of Texas will know that a Tennessean is the best marksman."

"Yes," Seguin replied, "and all of Tennessee will know that a Texan is not only the best horsemen, but also the best marksman."

Crockett smiled. "Tomorrow will bring the light of truth."

*   *   *

Lieutenant Colonel Travis was again looking for a volunteer courier. Travis previously made this request seven times, and each time one brave man stepped forward. None of them had returned. The Mexican lines were apparently too strong to break through.

This time, no one volunteered for Travis' call.

Travis pondered his next move, and concluded there was one man in the ranks who was best suited for his latest assignment. He called on Captain Seguin to ride to Goliad.

Seguin, Travis reasoned, had the best chance to secure help for the besieged garrison. Seguin knew the language. He knew the hostile Texas terrain. And, most of all, there was no one better on the back of a horse.

Travis was certain Seguin could break through the Mexican lines unharmed and reach Col. James Fannin at Goliad. Ride for Goliad, Travis asked Seguin, and recruit any and every man to help defend the Alamo.

Seguin hesitated. Not out of fear, but honor.

Travis listened as the brave *Tejano* tried to explain his position. Seguin told Travis he represented all Texans — native or not — and that he felt bound to finish the fight he had helped start. Futhermore, Seguin concluded, "My prize horse was shot and I have no horse to ride."

Jim Bowie, a trusted friend of Seguin, interrupted.

"*Amigo*," Bowie said to Seguin, "you have complimented me on my horse on many occasions. My horse is yours to ride. Ride like the wind. Recruit any and all help possible to help save the day."

Seguin nodded in agreement.

Bowie's horse was retrieved and saddled for Seguin, who received his final instructions from Travis. Goodbyes were now in order.

Crockett was the last to shake Seguin's hand. Saying goodbye was tough, but Crockett, as usual, found the words. He wished his new friend good fortune and safety.

As Seguin straddled Bowie's horse, Crockett reached up and shook Seguin's hand one last time and said, "Don't you forget, we still have a shooting match to attend to. So don't go and get yourself killed."

Raising his hand in the air, Crockett gave Bowie's horse a swift swat on the rump and shouted, "Open the gate for there goes a brave and true Texan!"[12]

Seguin made it safely through the Mexican lines, and immediately rallied reinforcements to ride to the aid of his friends in the Alamo.

By February 28, Seguin was camped on the Cibolo River waiting to join Col. James W. Fannin and his forces from Goliad. They waited in vain. Fannin never came, and Seguin soon heard news of the Alamo's fall.

Seguin left no doubt about his feelings toward the men at the Alamo.

One year later, on February 25, Seguin shared those feelings at a burial ceremony in Bexar for the Alamo's defenders. He eloquently stated that the defenders "chose to offer their lives to the ferocity of the enemy."

SAMUEL A. MAVERICK

Home with a View

The following story is based on oral evidence from Ellen Maverick Dickson and Rena M. Green's "Memoirs of Mary A. Maverick: San Antonio's First American Woman." Dickson is a great-granddaughter of Mary and Samuel A. Maverick, who represented the Alamo garrison at the Washington-on-the-Brazos Independence Convention.

Samuel A. Maverick never really found the words to describe his feelings for those who died at the Alamo. Words always fell short.

So he expressed himself through action.

Maverick moved his family into a new, two-story home on a lot in the northwest corner of Alamo Plaza in 1850.

Mary Maverick, his tall and beautiful wife,[13] recalled that exciting day in her memoirs:

> December 1st, 1850. We moved into our new house and found it very nice, after the old Mexican quarters we had occupied over a year.[14]

Mr. Maverick was especially fond of the new homestead's location. In a July 3, 1847, letter to Capt. S. M. Howe, Maverick first expressed his real interest behind that one lot when he wrote,

> I have a desire to reside on this particular spot, a foolish prejudice no doubt as I was almost a solitary escapee from the Alamo massacre having been sent by those unfortunate men to represent them in the independence convention.[15]

Many of the Alamo's men were his friends, such as Lieutenant Colonel Travis, whom he greatly admired. There was also the gallant James Butler Bonham, with whom Maverick practiced law for a year in Pendleton, South Carolina. These were great men. These were men who died for a belief — Maverick's belief — and men who put their faith in him.

Four *Tejanos* were elected by the citizens of Bexar to represent them at the Washington-on-the-Brazos Independence Convention. The citizens excluded those within the Alamo from the vote, regarding them as transients.

Alamo defenders thus held their own election. They chose Jesse Badgett and the popular Maverick.

As sobering as the thought was in his later years, the election saved Maverick's life.

On March 2, four days before the Mexican Army's final assault, Maverick departed the Alamo en route for Washington-on-the-Brazos. He never forgot the fateful moment he and Travis said goodbye.

Travis, it is believed, held Maverick back several days after Badgett's departure to use him as a messenger as well as a delegate. Now both men were staring at the moment of truth.

Travis leaned his head against Maverick's horse and urged his friend to send reinforcements.[16]

Help, of course, never arrived in time. But Maverick never forgot his friends or their sacrifice. For deep within his heart, where words struggled to emerge, he always remembered.

And in remembrance, the view from the front porch of Maverick's new home was chosen. His house faced the Alamo.

JAMES WILSON NICHOLS

Alamo Butcher?

The following sidebar is based on oral evidence presented by Donald Ottinger and James Wilson Nichols in "Now You Hear My Horn: The Journal of James Wilson Nichols 1820-1887." Ottinger is a great-grandson of Nichols. As a child he heard stories about his ancestor from his mother, Lula McDonald.

Generation after generation passed the story down with pride. There wasn't much to the story, but it didn't seem to matter. Old James Wilson Nichols had a role in the Alamo saga, and descendants were proud.

Nichols was a butcher at the Alamo. He slaughtered the beef for the garrison's now-immortal defenders, men like William Barret Travis, David Crockett, and James Bowie.

Then fate intervened.

Nichols was one of the men sent out of the Alamo to round up some more cattle. Upon his return to the garrison, he and his comrades were alarmed to find the Alamo encricled by the Mexican Army. There was no way to enter, and they knew the men inside were trapped.

Realizing they had no other course of action, Nichols and his companions reluctantly retreated from the Bexar area.[17]

Through the years, various descendants have tried to verify Nichols' presence at the Alamo, but without success. All they had was the family legend.

Then, on a November day in 1962, the undocumented story took on a strange new chapter. A thirteen-year-old girl, Sylvia Peters, entered the Daughters of the Republic of Texas Library at the Alamo and handed a librarian a tightly rolled sheaf of yellowed, stained, and torn papers. She said the old manuscript was the journal of her great-great-grandfather James Wilson Nichols.

Peters proceeded to tell the story of Nichols being a butcher at the Alamo.

The treasured journal, which has since been published,[18] doesn't support the family legend, although a number of pages are missing from the original documents. Nichols writes he crossed the Sabine River with his family into Texas on December 16, 1836. He was sixteen at the time.

Nichols also recounts a visit with his father and Johnson Day to San Antonio in the early part of 1837. Like many early travelers to Texas, Nichols was awestruck by his visit to the Alamo. He wrote:

> While thare I found a Mexican with old Davy Crockets gun and it was broak off at the bretch and it was a very noted gun. The naked barrel weighed 18 pounds with a plate of silver let into the barrel just behind the hind sight with the name Davy Crockette ingraved on it and another plate near the bretch with Drue Lane make ingraved on it, and thare was a young man with us claimed to be a son of Davy Crocketts baught the gun and carried it off home.

A year or two after that I was in San Antonio and found Crocketts cap mad out of a rackoon skin with the hair pulled out leaving only the fur and with a fox tail hanging down behind, also his shot pouch mad of panter-skin with the tail for a flap. . . .[19]

The diary seems to indicate Nichols was not at the Alamo during the siege. As editor Catherine W. McDowell wrote in the introduction of her book *Now You Hear My Horn: The Journal of James Wilson Nichols 1820–1887,* "from the way he wrote of other experiences, one would think that he would have said something about it if he had known Crockett previously."

"However," McDowell adds, "since the story of his having been at the Alamo comes from descendants who have not known each other and whose mutual ancestors are Jim Nichols and Milford Day, it must have some basis, to have been handed down in all branches of the family."

McDowell offers a possible explanation.

Andrew Sowell, Byrd Lockhart, and others were sent from the Alamo for provisions, and they were from the Gonzales area, where the Nichols family settled. Nichols' sister, Elizabeth, married John Sowell, Jr., and his father, George Washington Nichols, married Rachel Sowell, the mother of John and Andrew Sowell. Thus James Wilson Nichols and Andrew Sowell were both brothers-in-law and stepbrothers.

In telling the story through the years, McDowell suggests, these two could have been confused.

"As for the story, that's what it is, just a story," said Donald Ottinger, a great-grandson of Nichols. "I heard the story growing up. My mother said she heard the story growing up. But in his diary, he says himself he didn't cross the Sabine River into Texas until December 16, 1836.

"There were two Nichols families who entered Texas around that time, though. The family thinks the butcher may be an uncle, but we haven't been able to find anything to prove that. It's a mystery."

JAMES L. ALLEN

Last Hope

The following legend of Alamo courier James L. Allen is based on an F. C. Proctor interview with news reporter Robert H. Davis (date unknown). Proctor says he was fourteen years old when he heard the story from Allen, then a judge. Proctor claims the story was later ver- ified by Allen's daughter, Mary L. Cunningham.

Lieutenant Colonel Travis made it known to his men in the Alamo he needed another courier. Travis was determined to reach Col. James Fannin at Goliad with yet another plea. Fannin had to be convinced to come to the aid of the garrison with his troops.

Travis sensed time was running out. For twelve days, he and his men had been besieged by a superior force of Mexicans under the command of General Santa Anna. Only 189 men held the Alamo. The situation was desperate. Reinforcements had to arrive soon or the Alamo would be lost.

Several men volunteered on that March 5 afternoon to make the daring ride. Among them was James L. Allen.

The twenty-one-year-old Allen had left his home in Missouri with fellow classmates from Marion College in 1835. They were bound for the wilds of Texas, where prospects of a successful and adventurous life were rumored to be excellent.

Allen had volunteered for military service in Texas upon his arrival, and soon found himself in the middle of a revolution. Now he stood in front of Travis with other defenders awaiting the colonel's answer.

Travis told Allen he would be the one to make the attempt to carry the message to Fannin because he had the fleetest mare.

Shortly after nightfall, Allen grabbed the reins on the bridle of his horse and mounted bareback. A gate was opened and off he rode. Allen bent low and hugged the horse's neck, providing a lesser target as he dashed through the Mexican lines. Every bul- let missed its mark as Allen disappeared out of sight toward the east.

After roughly two days of hard riding, Allen arrived in Goliad some ninety-five miles from the Alamo. When he found Fannin unable to comply with the request, Allen quickly rode to Gonzales, arriving on March 11.

Anselmo Borgara arrived in Gonzales from a ranch near Bexar at about the same time. He informed Allen and others of the gory details regarding the fall of the Alamo on March 6.

Borgara said the Texans — 182 in all — had been massacred to the last man. He went on to report some 521 Mexicans died in the battle and as many were wounded.

At that moment, Allen realized he owed his life to his horse. He had narrowly escaped death as the Alamo's last courier.[20]

TAPLEY HOLLAND

Cross the Line

The following story is based on W. P. Zuber's "Sketch of Tapley Holland: A Heroe of the Alamo, March 6, 1836." Zuber claims to base the sketch on firsthand knowledge and conversations with Holland's sister, Nancy Berryman.

W. P. Zuber enjoyed rehashing those early days of adventure in Texas. He served in the campaign for independence, and the stories were always close to his heart.

Chatting with early pioneer Nancy Berryman was thus a treat for the colorful Zuber. One of Berryman's brothers, Tapley Holland, had died at the Alamo. Holland was no ordinary Texas pioneer. He was in many ways bigger than life, and when Berryman and Zuber talked at length, the legend grew . . .

*   *   *

Torn and ragged clothes hung on Tapley Holland as he moved about the Alamo, working to secure its defense against the counterattack expected by the Mexican Army. Measles spread throughout the garrison, and for a time Holland was strapped with the disease. Now he just wanted some rest.

Holland had been in the field since the autumn of 1835, ever since the settlers in Austin's Colony heard of the Texian skirmish with Mexican troops near the town of Gonzales. He and his brothers, James and Frank, were quick to volunteer. They marched westward before joining the frontier army.

The pace of war proved to be frantic.

With March of 1836 closing in, Holland had already seen action in the Battle of Concepcion, the Grass Fight, and the Siege and Battle of Bexar. Another clash with the Mexican Army seemed inevitable.

At Concepcion, the Hollands and 88 other Texians fought off 400 Mexicans and captured their cannon. Only one Texan died in the confrontation, but James Holland shortly thereafter fell victim to the spread of measles and a cold, which settled into his lungs. Too sick to fight, James was eventually taken back to the Holland homestead in Grimes County by Frank to recover. Both men vowed to return as soon as James was back on his feet.

Tapley, meanwhile, carried on the fight with his trusty Yeager rifle.

Following the storming of Bexar, Tapley was one of the few men who remained in the Alamo under Col. James C. Neill. Holland saw the colonel eventually relinquish his command to Lieutenant Colonel Travis when Neill returned home due to illness.

Weary and dirty, Tapley Holland still had more than enough fight to give.

He was a true frontiersman, raised on the hunt and the philosophy that only the strong survive. His father and mother were among Stephen F. Austin's original 300 settlers, and Tapley inherited some of that same spirit. He was as rugged and as tough as the next Texian, and he had the stories to prove his grit.

Once, while hunting on the prairie, Holland came upon a herd of magnificent bucks. Realizing he was too far away to get off an accurate shot, he quietly dropped to his knees and crawled through the tall grass, concealing himself from the unsuspecting animals.

Wavering grass ahead instantly put Holland on defense. He

soon realized he was in the presence of Indians, who were between himself and the herd of bucks.

Holland, certain he was heading into a trap, leaped to his feet. Eight Indians suddenly appeared from the tall grass, each gazing at Holland as he gripped his Yeager rifle. Three of the Indians also held rifles, and they waved Holland forward, only to be rejected.

Holland wasn't about to trust any Indian.

Instead, Holland turned around and started to retreat toward his camp. The sound of gunfire echoed overhead and Holland wheeled back toward the Indians with his loaded rifle. He estimated the distance between them to be roughly 180 yards.

Taking careful aim, Holland discharged his rifle and lodged a bullet into the chest of one of the Indians. The Indian dropped dead. Realizing Holland's rifle was empty, the other seven Indians let out piercing screams and charged. Holland retreated, loading his rifle on the run. He again wheeled and fired at the onrushing Indians, this time from approximately seventy yards. Holland again hit his mark and another Indian fell dead.

But the Indians closed in rapidly.

By this time, Holland's traveling companion, Robert Moffett, heard the commotion and came rushing over with his gun. Holland grabbed the gun and picked off a third Indian from ten yards away. A hand-to-hand fight to the finish appeared inevitable, but to the good fortune of Holland and Moffett, the Indians decided to retreat. Holland quickly reloaded his rifle and fired, wounding a fourth Indian as the shaken group scampered out of sight.

So what could a few Mexicans do?

Holland didn't seem to care. Rest and a clean outfit seemed foremost on his mind. After all, he had been wearing the same two suits since he joined the Texas Army in the autumn. His clothes were now filthy, tattered, and hardly warm.

War was certainly testing his toughness.

Holland made it a point to send a message with his cousin, John Peterson, prior to his departure from the Alamo. Peterson was one of the last men who left the garrison alive.

"I shall never leave this garrison 'till it shall become strong enough to defend itself against the advancing enemy," Holland told Peterson. "Tell our friends to hasten on and relieve me. I want to go home, rest a while, and procure some clothes."

Relief never came.

By March 3, the Alamo's fate seemed clear. Thousands of Mexican troops under General Santa Anna surrounded the Alamo in a death grip.

Travis called his men together on that day during a recess from the enemy's continual bombardment. He told them he had lost all hope for aid, and that he was resolved to stay and die fighting. The charismatic Travis then drew a line in the dirt with the tip of his sword and invited anyone who wanted to stay and die for his country to step across the line.

Holland was the first to emerge from the ranks.

The rough-and-tumble frontiersman stepped across the line and declared, "I am ready to die for my country."

All but one of his fellow comrades followed Holland's lead. Three days later, Holland died as he requested.[21]

LOUIS "MOSES" ROSE

Live or Die

Pat Baimbridge presented the oral evidence for the following story. Baimbridge is a great-great-great-nephew of Alamo defender Louis "Moses" Rose, and he grew up hearing stories about his famous ancestor from his grandmother, Ethylene Janelle Rose Baimbridge.

Old man Louis "Moses" Rose couldn't sleep. The cannon blasts from the Mexican Army had momentarily subsided, but his presence in the besieged Alamo gnawed at his heart.

Rose was no stranger to war. He had fought with Napoleon as a French mercenary at Waterloo, and received the French Legion of Honor for his courageous actions in battle. Hand-to-hand combat, the thrust of a bayonet, flying grapeshot, massive death . . . Rose had seen it all.

Waterloo seemed like ages ago, though.

Rose was now sixty-two years old. He had fought his war, and the thought of living out the rest of his life sounded mighty appealing. Yet there was the cause — Texas independence — and his good friend, Jim Bowie, to think of.

Ol' Jim Bowie. If it hadn't been for Bowie, Rose figured he probably wouldn't even be in the Alamo.

Bowie and Rose were very fond of each other. They met years earlier when Bowie was traveling through Nacogdoches toward the Texas–Louisiana border. Trouble was brewing down on the border, and Bowie was going to set matters straight.

Rose took an instant liking to Bowie. So Rose figured he would tag along.

Bowie, Rose, and ten (or twelve) other men went on to capture a Mexican garrison. Their small band held their position until authorities arrived.

Rose and Bowie never shied away from trouble. If there was a scrap, and they thought right was on their side, they were there. No questions asked.

Yet their friendship wasn't based solely on the next battle they could find. Hardly. Rose could never forget the rip-roaring times they had on their trips to New Orleans. Drinks, women, and money were bountiful in New Orleans, and Rose and Bowie were smack dab in the middle of it all whenever they visited a certain pub. Only the wealthiest in New Orleans frequented the establishment, which served as a popular meeting place and business hub. Landowners and slave traders from the region often used the pub as a place to make their deals.

Pirate Jean Lafitte would even make regular appearances to auction his slaves at the pub. Like many of the tavern's patrons, Lafitte was a good friend of both Bowie and Rose. In fact, many of those patrons had donated money to help support the revolution in Texas.

At the Alamo, Rose couldn't stop thinking about life. He and the other Alamo defenders talked frequently about life and death. Most, Rose believed, knew the gravity of their situation. If reinforcements didn't arrive soon — and that was looking like a lost cause — all would perish from another full assault by the Mexican Army.

The Alamo defenders had gallantly held off the Mexicans

Sketch of Moses Rose pondering his decision to stay or leave.
— Sketch by Gary Zaboly

thus far, but Rose knew the odds were stacking against them with each passing hour. Rose was a seasoned war veteran, and when he looked around the Alamo compound, all he saw was a "bunch of farmers."

Time was running out. Rose knew he had to make a decision, and his friends said the time has come to get out while there was still a chance. He agreed.

Besides, Rose was tired of fighting. For his entire life, it seemed, all he had done was fight. Now was the time to live.

Rose grabbed his pistol, gathered some of the garrison's women and children, and slipped over one of the Alamo walls with them in the cover of darkness. Miraculously, they escaped through the Mexican lines. Rose's dark complexion helped him pass freely through the countryside.

General Houston would eventually praise Rose for his daring escape, and for taking women and children to safety. A bounty of land accompanied the praise.

But Rose didn't escape the Alamo completely unscathed. Cactus, which littered the Texas prairie, battered his legs on his desperate flight back to Nacogdoches. Years later, Rose found himself constantly nagged by chronic leg problems. Infections set in and never went away. Those problems eventually sent him to his grave.

Rose was buried on a plantation just across the Texas border in Louisiana.

Even more nagging than the chronic leg problems, however, was the issue of Rose's departure from the Alamo garrison. Friends, neighbors, and casual acquaintances always asked Rose why he left. They always wanted to know why he didn't stay and die with the rest of the Alamo's brave combatants.

The answer was rather simple for the old French mercenary. Rose always told them, "By God, I wasn't ready to die."[22]

JAMES BUTLER BONHAM

Suicide Ride

The basis for the following story was taken from Milledge Louis Bonham's The Life and Times of Milledge Luke Bonham *and a* Dallas Morning News *article written in 1931 by Jan Isbelle Fortune called "Why Bonham Chose To Die With Travis." Bonham was the older brother of Alamo defender James Butler Bonham.*

Fortune's article, while obviously laced with romance and heroism, was nonetheless taken from family accounts passed down to Mrs. Edger Wade, a great-great-great-niece of the Alamo hero.

Guilt followed Milledge Luke Bonham to his deathbed. He never forgave himself for lending his brother, James, the necessary funds for a trip to Texas.

The trip led James Butler Bonham into the unrest of the Texas territory and ultimately to his death at the Alamo on March 6, 1836. James, one year shy of thirty, first entertained thoughts of Texas when he received word from William Barret Travis, a childhood friend, of the new, glorious land.

Travis, a lieutenant colonel in the Texas army, urged Bonham to join him if he sought adventure and a place to build a fortune. Texas was on the verge of something exciting, Travis predicted.

Bonham was sold.

The impulsive Bonham closed his law practice in Montgomery, Alabama, and returned to South Carolina to help raise funds for his Texas journey. Milledge's contribution gave James the necessary sum to make the fateful trip.

In later years, Milledge often wondered what might have been had he not given James the money. The burden weighed heavily on his heart.

Milledge did have one consoling thought. In exchange for his life, James attained immortality as an Alamo defender.

Texans hailed the dashing James Butler Bonham as a hero. Yet Milledge wouldn't learn the full extent of his brother's heroism until two years after his death.

In 1838, Milledge traveled to Texas to learn of his brother's final days. He interviewed General Houston, two companions who rode with James to the Alamo, and Susanna Dickinson, who, along with her baby, were the only Anglo survivors in the battle.

Gathering as much information as possible, Milledge returned home with a story that would make relatives weep with pride. He would tell of James Butler Bonham's suicide ride . . .

* * *

Hopes were high within the walls of the Alamo when Travis called on his old friend, Bonham, to ride for help. Reports of the Mexican Army's advance across the Rio Grande had already reached Bexar, and Travis was seeking more reinforcements.

Col. James Walker Fannin commanded several hundred troops at Goliad, and was thus the most likely source for relief. So Bonham rode.

Fannin refused to answer Bonham's impassioned plea for help. The young South Carolinian, after begging Fannin to reconsider, was finally resolved to report the bad news to Travis that Fannin would not budge.

Two companions rode alongside Bonham on his journey back to Bexar, where they discovered the Alamo's desperate situation. From a hill overlooking Bexar, the three couriers saw the Alamo surrounded by hundreds of Mexican campsites. Thousands of Mexican soldiers had the mission choked off to the rest of Texas.

Still, Bonham told his two companions he must deliver Fannin's message to Travis. His two comrades urged Bonham to retreat with them, realizing the fate of the Alamo was already sealed. Any other decision, the two argued, would be suicidal.

Bonham replied in a Southern drawl, "I will report the result of my mission to Travis or die in the attempt."

His two companions knew Bonham was serious. They wished him luck, wheeled their horses around, and rode away.

Bonham was serious. Chivalry was in his blood.

He was committed to the cause of Texas liberty, and left no doubts about his loyalties in a letter to General Houston from San Felipe, December 1, 1835.

"Permit me, through you to volunteer my services in the present struggle of Texas without conditions," wrote Bonham. "I shall receive nothing, either in the form of service pay, or lands or rations."[23]

Now, months later, Bonham surveyed the Alamo's desperate situation from a hilltop. He proceeded to tie a white handkerchief to his hat. He prayed his comrades along the Alamo walls would recognize the symbol and hold their gunfire — if he made it that far.

Bonham then spurred his trusty, dove-colored horse and made a dash for the Alamo. He clung low to his steed and slid to one side as a Comanche would, while Mexican soldiers scurried about at the alarming thud of hoofbeats.

A hail of gunshots whizzed overhead. A gate swung open as Bonham and his horse drew closer to the Alamo, and he soon sped inside to the dubious safety of the compound.

Miraculously, Bonham was unharmed.[24]

What hurt Bonham the most was the news he carried. He knew his words were as good as poison.

Travis hugged his friend and eagerly asked about his findings. Was help on the way? Bonham looked his friend in the eyes.

"There is no help coming, Will," Bonham said sadly. "No help . . . for the Alamo . . ."[25]

On the night before the final assault, Bonham joined Susanna and Almeron Dickinson for some tea. They enjoyed one another's company, and undoubtedly pondered their future.

The next morning, following a monumental struggle with the Mexicans, Almeron Dickinson and Bonham were found dead, lying near their artillery post in the chapel.

A part of Milledge died that day too.[26]

JUANA NAVARRO DE ALSBURY

Protector

Oral evidence for the following story was presented by Dorothy Perez, a great-granddaughter of Alamo survivor Alijo Perez, Jr. She heard the story at the age of twelve from her aunt, Mamie Sosa.

Survival was foremost on Juana Navarro de Alsbury's mind in the early morning hours of March 6, 1836. She hovered over her eleven-month-old son, Alejo Perez, Jr., when the blast of cannon and the crack of gunfire grew louder and louder.

Soon she would hear the horrifying screams of hand-to-hand combat as Mexican soldiers poured into the Alamo compound to engage the defiant Texians.

De Alsbury had taken refuge in the Alamo along with her son and sister, Gertrudis Navarro, when the siege began February 23. She had been married for only about a month when her second husband, Dr. Horace Alsbury, left Bexar on a scouting mission.

Saving Alejo, Jr., was now her only priority.

Sometime before the final assault, Juana and her companions in the Alamo chapel slipped a dress on her son to make him look like a girl. She figured it might be the only way of getting Alijo out of the Alamo alive.

Whether or not the ploy helped, Juana and her son were released after the battle.[27]

Antonio López de Santa Anna
— Courtesy Forest View Historical Services

JACOB WALKER

Final Message

The following story is based on oral evidence presented by Jessie Mc-Ilroy Smith, as well as Smith's "Sarah Vauchere Walker's 70 Years on the Texas Frontier." Smith is a great-granddaughter of Sarah Ann Vauchere and Jacob Walker, an Alamo artilleryman.

The Nacogdoches crowd grew restless with anxiety over the latest news. With the Mexican Army storming into Texas on a trail of blood from the South, now came word Indians would join the fight. Reliable sources claimed local tribes were planning to join Mexican General Santa Anna and would attempt to ambush the Texian Army from the rear.

Those in attendance knew the grave importance of such a threat. Few believed the struggling Texian Army could withstand a surprise attack, and the buzz from the crowd grew louder and louder. How could they avoid a potential massacre by joint Mexican and Indian forces?

Texians were already digging in for a fight at Bexar and Goliad, and somewhere between Nacogdoches and Bexar, General Houston was scrounging up an army.

Suggestions were shouted from all corners of the meeting room before order was finally restored. A decision had been made. All agreed a volunteer was needed to carry this crucial news to Houston.

The life of Texas hung in the balance.

A woman with golden hair and blue eyes, and standing at a mere four feet eight inches, stepped forward. She was Sarah Ann Vauchere Walker, and she spoke in broken English with a French accent.

"I will go," she said without hesitation.

Walker said Houston was a friend of the family. Besides, Walker reasoned she could ride a horse as well as a Comanche warrior, and her ability to speak French on the frontier would save her should she encounter any Native Americans on her journey. Texas Indians were known to be friendly with the few remaining French in the territory.

Walker's determination won out. All agreed she would carry the message.

Walker's will to fight belied her aristocratic upbringing. She received her education as a member of the Mississippi French aristocracy in the early 1800s, and it was there she refined her grace and charm. She spoke both French and Latin, but wrote neither because it wasn't appropriate for a French woman to write at that time.

Beautiful clothes, jewelry, and other luxurious objects were her weakness. Family members recalled she would give up ridiculous amounts of cotton or stock or slaves for items of glamour.[28]

But now she was ready to put her life on the line with a daring ride across the Texas frontier.

War was slowly teaching Walker something she hadn't learned as a member of the Mississippi French aristocracy. In Texas, she was learning about survival.

Walker's husband, Jacob, was already knee-deep in the revolution. The thirty-seven-year-old Jacob had followed the route of his old friend, Houston, and volunteered to fight for Texas independence. He had joined the army and was stationed in Bexar in Capt. William R. Carey's artillery company at a mission fortress called the Alamo.[29]

Like the famous David Crockett and James Bowie, reputation preceded most of the men into the Alamo. Although many had never met, they all knew each other through hearsay and regional stories. Jacob Walker was well known in Nacogdoches, where he had eventually settled after marrying Sarah Ann and disposing of land in Natchitoches, Louisiana, in 1827.

He was as tough as the next man.

Little did Jacob know that Sarah Ann was building her own reputation.

Sarah Ann dressed like a boy and rode out of Nacogdoches with news of an Indian ambush. She rode for roughly 300 miles before finally reaching Houston. As expected, her French tongue allowed her to slip past many Indian checkpoints along her route.[30]

The heroic ride of the tiny French woman through the tur-

Sketch of Jacob Walker's final moment.
— Drawing by Gary Zaboly

bulent frontier saved the army from disaster, and Houston was forever indebted to his old friend.

Years later, Houston would regularly visit with Sarah Ann and stay the night at her plantation. Houston always drank too much during those visits, but was still highly respected by Sarah Ann and her family. After all, he, too, put his life on the line for Texas, and talk would almost always shift to those adventurous days of the glorious revolution.

Houston never forgot Sarah Ann's great ride. Nor did he forget his old friend, Jacob, who perished in the Alamo on March 6, 1836.

Everyone enjoyed remembering Jacob Walker. He died with honor, and he died remembering his family. The story of his final moments never grew tiresome in family circles.

Walker had helped man one of the Alamo cannon above the chapel throughout most of the siege. In the frenzy of the final assault, Walker was wounded and staggered to the ground level of the chapel to find Susanna Dickinson, whose husband, Almeron, was one of Jacob's artillery officers.

Walker stumbled into the room where Mrs. Dickinson and her baby were hiding, and tried to give her a message for his wife. But several Mexican soldiers cornered Walker and plunged their bayonets into his body. The Mexicans then hoisted Walker overhead, like a pitchfork of hay, and discharged their rifles into his body.[31]

HENRY WARNELL

Daring Escape

Oral evidence for this story was presented by Kevin L. Wornell, who has gathered various family legends over the years. Wornell once interviewed a distant cousin, Eydith Wornell Roach, who related the story of Alamo defender Henry Warnell's travels into Texas. Wornell believes he is a distant relative of Warnell, but has never been able to prove it with documentation.

Horses were scarce in Texas in the 1830s, making it just the place for Henry Warnell of Arkansas. Warnell was a wheeler and a dealer in the horse business. For the record, he dealt in stolen horses.

Folks called Warnell a jockey, and not merely for his ability to ride a thoroughbred. He knew horses, talked about them all the time, and more important to his livelihood, knew where to find buyers for his stolen horses.

Warnell took horses from Tennessee and Kentucky down to Texas along the "Midnight Trail."

In 1835 Warnell became a resident of Bastrop, Texas, where he hooked up with Edward Burleson. Warnell lived with Burleson and tended his horses.

Patriotism was the last thing stirring deep within Warnell when Texans began to take up arms against Mexican dictator Santa Anna in the momentous year of 1835. Described as "small, weighing less than 118 lbs., blue-eyed, red-headed, freckled and an incessant tobacco chewer," Warnell was remembered by family members as being a rogue and an outlaw.[32]

In time, perhaps through his association with the patriotic Burleson, Warnell found himself in the Alamo with other Texas revolutionaries.

Susanna Dickinson would recall a man at the Alamo named "Wornell" years later in sworn testimony before the Court of Claims:

> I knew a man there by the name of Wornell; and recollect distinctly having seen him in the Alamo about three days before its fall, and as none escaped the massacre I verily believe he was among the unfortunate number who fell in the defense of their country. I recollect having heard him remark that he would much rather be out on the open prairie, than to be pent up in this manner.[33]

Family legend states Warnell would find that open prairie one last time.

On the morning of March 6, according to legend, when the fighting became the most desperate, Warnell bolted over one of the compound walls with three other men. The two other men were killed by Mexican cavalry, while Warnell managed to escape despite being wounded.

Warnell's toughness was severely tested over the next couple of days. Bleeding greatly from his wound, he managed to hide during the day and travel at night before reaching Port Lavaca. His night travel left his legs scarred, as he scraped against dense brush and the thorny mesquite of the Texas prairie.

Warnell died later that year, in June, at Port Lavaca.[34] He died with the distinction of being the only defender to leave the battle alive.[35]

ENRIQUE ESPARZA

Eyewitness to Hell

Alamo survivor Enrique Esparza's story is told through the following excerpts taken from a 1907 San Antonio Express *article entitled "Alamo's Only Survivor."*

Pupils at Bowie School in San Antonio watched the old Mexican gentleman enter their classroom. He wore a colorful *zarape* around his shoulders and held a large hat.

"*Buenas dias, niños,*" the gentleman said.

"I am so glad you could come, *Señor* Esparza," said the teacher, extending her hand.

The teacher turned back to her class and introduced Enrique Esparza, survivor of the Battle of the Alamo. "This, boys and girls, is the man of whom I was just speaking . . . the boy of the Alamo. Won't you be seated, *Señor*?"

Esparza bowed and took a seat in front of the class.

In the following moments, Esparza would tell the students about his childhood experiences prior to the turn of the century in San Antonio de Bexar. He would speak of the poverty, the happiness, and finally the riveting story of the Alamo.[36]

Family members had often heard the story. Now Esparza

would share it with San Antonio's next generation. He was a witness to its horror at the age of twelve, and he felt a sense of duty to pass on his firsthand account.

Modestly, he would tell the class, "I wish I could tell you all the great bravery of these few Texans fighting against that host. It would take great words like in your Bible and in your songs. I do not know these words."[37]

Yet Esparza was a self-taught gentleman who spoke both Spanish and English with equal eloquence. If he did indeed struggle on occasion with his words, the Alamo story must have brought out something deep within.

For when he spoke of the Alamo and the men who died there, his words were captivating:

> All of the others are dead. I alone live of they who were within the Alamo when it fell. There is none other left now to tell its story and when I go to sleep my last slumber in the Campo de los Santos (cemetery), there will then be no one left to tell.
>
> You ask me do I remember it. I tell you, "Yes." It is burned into my brain and indellibly seared there. Neither age nor infirmity could make me forget, for the scene was one of such horror that it could never be forgotten by anyone who witnessed its incidents. . . .
>
> I was then a boy of 12 years of age; was then quite small and delicate and could have passed for a child of 8. My father was a friend and comrade of William Smith. Smith had expected to send my father and our family away with his own family in a wagon to Nacogdoches. We were waiting for the wagon to be brought to town. My father and Smith had heard of the approach of (General) Santa Anna, but did not expect him and his forces to arrive as early as they did. Santa Anna and his men got here before the wagon we waited for could come.
>
> My father was told by Smith that all who were friends to the Americans had better join the Americans who had taken refuge in the Alamo. Smith and his family went there and my father and his family went with them. . . .
>
> It was twilight when we got into the Alamo and it grew pitch dark soon afterward. All of the doors were closed and barred. The sentinels that had been on duty without were first called inside and then the openings were closed. Some sentinels were posted upon the roof, but these were protected by

the walls of the Alamo church and the old convent building. We went into the church portion. It was shut up when we arrived. We were admitted through a small window.

I distinctly remember that I climbed through the window and over a cannon that was placed inside of the church immediately behind the window. There were several other cannon there. Some were back of the doors. Some had been mounted on the roof and some had been placed in the convent. The window was opened to permit us to enter and it was closed immediately after we got inside.

We had not been in there long when a messenger came from Santa Anna calling on us to surrender. I remember the reply to this summons was a shot from one of the cannon on the roof of the Alamo. Soon after it was fired I heard Santa Anna's cannon reply. I heard his cannon shot strike the walls of the church and also the convent. Then I heard the cannon within the Alamo buildings, both the church and convent, fire repeatedly during the night. I heard the cheers of the Alamo gunners and the deriding jeers of Santa Anna's troops.

My heart quaked when the shot tore through the timbers. My fear and terror was overwhelming, but my brave mother and my dauntless father sought to soothe and quiet my brothers and myself. My sister was but an infant and knew not of the tragic scenes enacted about us. But even child as I was I could not help but feel inspired by the bravery of the heroes about me.

If I had been given a weapon I would have fought likewise. But weapons and ammunition were scarce and only wielded and used by those who knew how. But I saw some there no older than I who had them and fought as bravely and died as stolidly as the adults. This was towards the end and when many of the grown persons within had been slain by the foes without. It was then that some of the children joined in the defense.

All who had weapons used them as often as they had the chance to do so. Shots were fired fast. Bullets flew thick. Both men and women fell within the walls. Even children died there. The fighting was intermittent. We must have been within the Alamo 10 or 12 days. I did not count the days. But they were long and full of terror. The nights were longer and fraught with still more horror. It was between the periods of fierce fighting and all-too-short armistice that we got any rest.

[David] Crockett seemed to be the leading spirit. He was everywhere. He went to every exposed point and personally

directed the fighting. [William Barret] Travis was chief in command, but he depended more upon the judgment of Crockett
and that brave man's intrepidity than upon his own. [Jim]
Bowie, too, was brave and dauntless, but he was ill. Prone
upon his cot he was unable to see much that was going on
about him and the others were too engrossed to stop and tell
him. Although too weak to stand upon his feet, when Travis
drew the line with his sword Bowie and those around him
[brought] his cot across the line.

I heard a few Mexicans there call Crockett "Don Benito."
Afterward, I learned his name was David, but I only knew him
as "Don Benito."

One day when I went to where Bowie was lying on his cot
I heard him call those about him and say:

"All of you who desire to leave here may go in safety.
Santa Anna has just sent a message to Travis saying there will
be an armistice for three days to give us time to deliberate on
surrendering. During these three days all who desire to do so
may go out of here. Travis has sent me the message and told
me to tell those near me."

When Bowie said this, quite a number left. Travis and
Bowie took advantage of this occasion to send out for succor
they vainly hoped would come to the Alamo and those within
before it fell. . . .

[Louis "Moses"] Rose left after the armistice had expired
and after the others had been sent for succor. Rose went out
after Travis drew the line with his sword. He was the only man
who did not cross the line. Up to then he had fought as bravely as any man there. He stood by the cannon.

Rose went out during the night. They opened a window
for him and let him go. . . .

Bowie asked my father if he wished to go when the armistice of three days was on. My father replied: "No. I will stay and
die fighting." My mother then said: "I will stay by your side and
with our children die, too. They will soon kill us. We will not
linger in pain."

So we stayed. And so my father died, as he said, fighting. . . .

The end came suddenly and almost unexpectedly and
with a rush. It came at night and when all was dark save when
there was a gleam of light from the flash and flame of a fired
gun. Our men fought hard all day long. Their ammunition was
very low. That of many was entirely spent. Santa Anna must

have known this, for his men had been able during the day to make several breeches in the walls. Our men fought long and hard and well. But their strength was spent. . . .

After all had been dark and quiet for many hours and I had fallen into a profound slumber suddenly there was a terrible din. Cannon boomed. Their shot crashed through the doors and windows and the breeches in the walls. Then men rushed in on us. They swarmed among us and over us. They fired on us in vollies. They struck us down with their escopetas. In the dark our men groped and grasped the throats of our foemen and buried their knives into their hearts.

By my side was an American boy. He was about my own age but larger. As they reached us he rose to his feet. He had been sleeping, but like myself, he had been rudely awakened. As they rushed upon him he stood calmly and across his shoulders drew the blanket on which he had slept. He was unarmed. They slew him where he stood and his corpse fell over me. My father's body was lying near the cannon which he had tended. My mother with my baby sister was kneeling beside it. My brothers and I were close to her. I clutched her garments. Behind her crouched the only man who escaped and was permitted to surrender. His name was Brigido Guerrera.

As they rushed upon us the Mexican soldiers faltered as they saw a woman. My mother clasped her babe to her breast and closed her eyes. She expected they would kill her and her babe and me and my brothers. I thought so, too. My blood ran cold and I grew faint and sick. . . .

They took my mother, her babe, my brothers and I to another part of the building where there were other women and children all huddled. Another of the women had a babe at her breast. This was Mrs. [Susanna] Dickinson. There was an old woman in there. They called her Donna Petra. This was the only name I ever knew her by. With her was a young girl, Trinidad Saucedo, who was very beautiful. Mrs. [Juana Navarro de Alsbury] and her sister were there also and several other women, young girls and little boys. . . .

After the soldiers of Santa Anna had got in a corner all of the women and children who had not been killed in the onslaught, they kept firing on the men who had defended the Alamo. For fully a quarter of an hour they kept firing upon them after all of the defenders had been slain. It was pitch dark in the Eastern end of the structure and the soldiers of Santa Anna seemed to fear to go there even after firing from the

Constitutionalists from there had ceased. Santa Anna's men stood still and fired into the darkness and until someone brought lanterns.

The last I saw of my father's corpse was when one of them held his lantern above it and over the dead who lay about the cannon he had tended.[38]

JOSE GREGORIO ESPARZA

Christian Burial

Oral evidence for the following story was presented by George Bena-vides, a great-great-great-great-grandson of Alamo defender Jose Gregorio Esparza. Benavides heard stories about the Alamo hero from his grandmother, Margarita Sotelo Rosales, while growing up.

One by one, the survivors of the Alamo were brought before Mexican General Santa Anna. Women were crying, babies were screaming, and the hardships of war had only just begun. Friends and loved ones were lost in the grisly battle, which claimed hundreds of lives from both armies.

Tejanos from Bexar and Mexican soliders had already started the gruesome task of collecting the dead in and around the Alamo compound. Santa Anna ordered all the bodies of the Texians — Col. James Bowie, Col. David Crockett, and Lt. Col. William Barret Travis — to be burned. There were to be no Christian burials for those who took up arms against Mexico.

Santa Anna made it clear he did not want such deeds to go unpunished.

As for the survivors, Santa Anna wanted them to carry this message across the Mexican province of Tejas. Rebels would be punished. Before releasing them, however, he personally interviewed each survivor. Then he gave each two silver *pesos* and a blanket.

Survivor Ana Salazar Esparza had a special request. When

Enrique Esparza
— Courtesy the Esparza family

Esparza and her four children were brought before the Mexican general, she could only think of her gallant husband.

Jose Gregorio Esparza had brought his wife and family into the Alamo, and when offered the opportunity to leave by Bowie, he had firmly replied, "No, I will stay and die fighting."[39]

Ana Salazar would not forget.

She asked Santa Anna in Spanish, "Instead of the two silver *pesos* and blanket, may I bury my husband?"

Santa Anna was curious. "Why should I, being a great dictator, grant you this wish?"

"Because," Ana Salazar said, "my brother-in-law fights for your great army. His name is Francisco Esparza."

Santa Anna immediately told one of his orderlies to find Francisco Esparza and bring him over. The orderly promptly obliged.

Ana Salazar Esparza's story was true. Francisco Esparza was serving under Santa Anna.

Years later, Francisco would swear he was forced into service when Santa Anna and his troops stormed Bexar. In fear of being executed, he did as he was told.

Francisco's decision would ironically save his brother's body from the Alamo funeral pyre. Santa Anna granted Ana Salazar her wish.

With Francisco's help, she had Gregorio's body removed from the battlefield and buried.

Jose Gregorio Esparza was the only Alamo defender who was given a Christian burial.[40]

Francisco Esparza
— Courtesy the Esparza family

FRANCISCO ESPARZA

Forever Brothers

The following story is based on oral evidence presented by Richard D. Esparza, as well as Esparza's "Brother At Arms." Esparza is the great-great-great-grandson of Francisco Esparza, brother of Alamo defender Jose Gregorio Esparza and a member of the Leal Presidios Company of Bexar. Francisco, who sympathized with the Mexican Army, helped gather the bodies of the Alamo dead.

A thunderous boom rocked the tiny hut at the west end of Calle de Rivas, awakening Francisco Esparza from a deep sleep in the early morning hours of March 6, 1836. The young man arose from his bed, trying not to disturb his wife, Maria. He slowly made his way outside.

Emerging from his home, Francisco saw a bright glow cover the sky above the old Spanish mission called Alamo. Cannon roared . . . gunfire crackled . . . fires raged out of control.

The Mexican Army under General Santa Anna was making the final assault on the rebel Texian forces under Lieutenant Colonel Travis.

Francisco watched in a mournful silence.

For inside the besieged mission fortress, among those desperately and hopelessly fighting for their lives, was Francisco's brother, Gregorio. Francisco knew he would never see his brother alive again.

Maria soon joined Francisco, who felt her presence. She offered a tender touch. Yet Francisco just stared into the bright glow.

Tensions between Francisco and Gregorio had increased more and more ever since the autumn of the previous year. Rebel foreigners were pushing for independence from Mexico, and the mere thought made Francisco furious.

Like Santa Anna, Francisco believed in "Mexico . . . for the Mexicans." The vast numbers of *gringos* immigrating to Texas greatly concerned him. He opposed what he believed was a dilution of the Mexican culture in Texas, especially in Bexar.

With the exception of neighbor Jim Bowie, Francisco felt the *gringos* were rude, obnoxious people. Their women were just as bad. Insubordinate. Opinionated. They did not know their place as the Mexican women did.

Gregorio viewed *gringos* differently.

Texas, Gregorio believed, would someday in his lifetime become an independent, English-speaking country or part of the United States. Therefore, he welcomed the *gringos* and wanted to learn their language. He and his wife, Ana, even encouraged their children to learn English from their Anglo-American playmates.

War further divided the brothers.

Forces under Mexican General Martin Perfecto de Cos occupied Bexar in October of 1835. Francisco took his place among his countrymen as a member of the Leal Presidios Company of Bexar, a local Mexican militia unit.

Two months later, the rebel Texians overwhelmed Cos and his forces after a fierce standoff in Bexar. The Texians demanded that Cos and his soldiers leave Texas and never return. Members of the local Mexican militia were allowed to remain.

Francisco was among those who chose to stay in Bexar as Cos crossed the Rio Grande with his defeated army.

Francisco did not know that Gregorio was among those Texian rebels who participated in the Battle of Bexar. He was infuriated when he learned of his brother's role in the battle. Being friends with the *gringos* was one thing. Joining them in a fight against your own countrymen was another. This was unacceptable in Francisco's eyes.

Francisco was certain the rebels hadn't seen the last of the Mexican Army. He knew the army would return, and with a vengeance. Blood would be spilled. For this reason, Francisco distanced himself from anyone who fought against Cos, even Gregorio.

Never again would their relationship be the same.

The feud between Gregorio and Francisco would not include their families. Ana and Maria ensured that their children would not suffer from the political differences of their fathers. The women wanted all seven of the Esparza children to grow up together, and to always be able to count on one another.

From time to time, Gregorio, Ana, and their children would walk down to Francisco's and Maria's house for dinner. On other occasions, Gregorio and Ana would return the favor as hosts.

On a cold February day in 1836, when Ana and Gregorio were told Santa Anna had arrived with his army, they were alarmed to hear Enrique was still in the plaza playing with his brother, Manuel, and cousin Jose. Upon hearing the news, Gregorio and Francisco went to retrieve their children. Women and children fled from the streets, and a convoy of wagons headed out of town. The two brothers figured they were headed for the Alamo.

Gregorio and Francisco eventually spoke.

Would Gregorio join the *gringos* in the Alamo? Yes.

Francisco offered his home to Gregorio's children, but Ana would politely turn down the offer later that day. The family, Ana argued, would not be separated. Gregorio honored her wishes.

With little else to say, the two brothers embraced and said goodbye. Each knew deep down it would be the last.

A member of the Leal Presidios Company of Bexar visited Francisco's home shortly after Gregorio's departure. By orders of Santa Anna, Francisco and other members of the company were to be on standby. Francisco realized he could be called to active duty at a moment's notice, and the thought disturbed him greatly.

Yet Francisco knew he had no choice.

* * *

Francisco continued to sit quietly as he watched the battle slowly come to an end. He saw the movement of the Mexican troops and heard the sporadic gunfire, thinking only of Gregorio's fate.

In the distance he saw the sunrise marking the dawn of a new day. Francisco turned and went back inside his house.

Several hours later, a young *soldado* called on Francisco and informed him of the Alamo's fall at 6:00 A.M. With the exception of a few women and children, the *soldado* said, there were no survivors.

Francisco fought back the tears.

The messenger then told Francisco the Leal Presidios Com-

pany of Bexar was being ordered to report for duty at 3:00 P.M.
The company would help in the burial of the brave Mexican soldiers who died for their country.

As for the Texans? Francisco was told they were to be cremated.

Francisco again tried to fight back the tears. The thought of
his brother's body being carelessly tossed into a funeral pyre was
too disturbing for him to take. He decided he would search for
Gregorio's body and ask permission to give him a Christian
burial.

As Francisco prepared to leave for the Alamo, his brothers,
Antonio and Victor, rode up. Emotions stirred when Francisco
broke the news of Gregorio's almost-certain death. The moment
seemed unreal.

How could this have happened? Why wasn't anyone able to
stop him?

With no easy answers to find, the three brothers rode for
the Alamo to find Gregorio's body.

Mangled, bloody bodies littered the outside of the mission
fortress as the Esparza brothers rode closer. They were sickened
at the ghastly sight, and paused briefly before entering the bat-
tle-scarred mission fortress.

Inside, they stepped carefully to avoid the hundreds of
corpses which lay strewn across the Alamo compound. Fixated
on the horrifying scene, the brothers began to wander around
the compound in a daze, scanning constantly for Gregorio.

The Esparza brothers eventually entered the Alamo chapel,
where they abruptly halted. For there at the far end of the chapel, at the base of the ramp along the east wall, lay Gregorio's
bloody and broken body.

Next to Gregorio lay the breathless bodies of his comrades,
Capt. Almeron Dickinson and James Butler Bonham.

Francisco, Victor, and Antonio slowly moved toward Gregorio's body. Standing before Gregorio's corpse, Francisco dropped
to his knees and quietly wept. Victor and Antonio also began to
cry. Prayers followed as the three brothers mourned together.

Suddenly, a voice startled them.

"Have you not been assigned any duties?" the voice asked.

Francisco and his brothers looked up from Gregorio's body

to discover they were in the presence of General Cos. They leaped to their feet and saluted.

"Yes, Excellency," Francisco nervously replied.

"Then why haven't you begun?"

"Because, Excellency," Francisco said, "this man here is my younger brother, Gregorio Esparza."

Cos dismounted his horse and approached the body. He examined the wounds and offered his sympathies. As Cos began to walk back to his horse, Francisco spoke up.

"Excuse me, Excellency," Francisco said. "I know that my brother has disgraced his country with his collaboration with the *gringos*, but I would consider it a great personal favor if you would allow me to bury him with the rites of our church."

Cos thought for a moment and then nodded his head.

"Thank you, your Excellency," Francisco said. "Thank you."

Victor and Francisco scooped up Gregorio's body and began to carry him out of the chapel. Francisco stopped for a moment in the middle of the chapel to inspect the familiar face of a Mexican *soldado*. Francisco looked closely.

The *soldado* was Ignacio Morales of Laredo, an old friend of Francisco's in the Mexican Army. Francisco lowered his head in grief.

Had Gregorio and his old friend confronted one another before their deaths?

Francisco didn't choose to torture himself any longer. He rose again to his feet and carried on as Gregorio's blood dripped on his clothes.

Corpses of Mexicans and Texans lay everywhere, and for the first time, Francisco began to question his own beliefs. Was Santa Anna's thirst for revenge worth the deaths of his brother and so many brave men on both sides of the battle? Was Santa Anna deserving of praise? Or was he just a savage tyrant?

Questions kept attacking Francisco as he and his brothers transported Gregorio's body by wagon to Plaza de las Islas and the San Fernando Church. Upon their arrival, they cried out for Padre de la Garza, who would perform the last rites according to the Catholic church.

Francisco, Victor, and Antonio found comfort in knowing their brother would receive a Christian burial.

Padre de la Garza instructed that Gregorio's body be taken to the San Fernando Campos Santos Cemetery, roughly a quarter mile south of the church. Gregorio was placed in the wagon.

The Esparza brothers followed on horseback, side by side, as a family.[41]

BENJAMIN HIGHSMITH

View from Powder House Hill

The following story is based on a memorial to Alamo courier Benjamin Highsmith written by his daughters, Martha Jane (Highsmith) O'Brien and Mary Deborah (Highsmith) O'Brien.

Young Benjamin Highsmith was summoned by Lieutenant Colonel Travis shortly after scouts reported the close proximity of Mexican General Santa Anna and his army. The decreasing distance between the Mexican Army and the Alamo was suddenly alarming.

Travis entrusted Highsmith with an urgent message for Col. James Fannin to abandon his position at Goliad and rush to the aid of the Alamo at once. Highsmith glanced at Travis as he jumped on his horse and took off to the southeast toward Goliad.

Mexican and Indian scouts were on his trail, but Highsmith dodged them in the muddy Texas terrain and reached Goliad safely to deliver the message. He promptly received Fannin's refusal to aid the Alamo, and five days later, returned to Powder House Hill where he halted his horse.

From Powder House Hill, Highsmith looked down on the Alamo, La Villita, and all of Bexar. The scene was tragic.

Fellow Texians still patrolled the walls of the Alamo and their flag still bravely waved in defiance. Yet it was plain to see that the defenders were cut off from the rest of the world as Mexican cavalry surrounded the compound. He also saw the blood-red flag of the Mexican Army waving from the top of San Fernando Church between Main and Military plazas.

Mexican soldiers spotted Highsmith as he took in the scene. They rode toward him at a furious pace.

Realizing his beloved commander and his comrades were doomed, Highsmith spurred his horse and bolted for Gonzales. The Mexicans chased Highsmith for six miles before giving up pursuit.

Highsmith eventually came to rest eighteen miles from the Alamo at the Cibolo River, where he watered his tired horse. Suddenly, he heard the thundering boom of the first cannon. The siege of the Alamo had begun.

The eighteen-year-old Highsmith reached Gonzales, where he immediately reported to General Houston, who was greatly distressed by the news of the siege and Fannin's failure to comply with Travis' desperate request for help.

General Houston then sent Highsmith and fellow youngster David Kent to Goliad with a second message for Fannin. They dashed off toward Goliad, delivered the message, and returned to Gonzales with a reply for General Houston.

Susanna Dickinson, the lone Anglo adult to survive the Alamo battle, preceded their return to Gonzales with news of the garrison's fall. Highsmith was told every defender in the Alamo, including Kent's father, Andrew, had been killed in the final assault on the morning of March 6.

Highsmith soon realized he was the last person to see Travis and the men of the Alamo alive.[42]

TRINIDAD COY

Loco Weed

The following passage is from an article published in the San Antonio Light, *November 26, 1911. The article is based on an interview with Andres Coy, a local policeman, who claimed his father, Trinidad, was sent from the Alamo to ascertain Santa Anna's position and intentions.*

But for the unguarded action of a farmer's boy, the history of Texas and the map of the United States might today be different.

When Travis, Bowie and Crockett and their band of immortal heroes lay intrenched in the Alamo in April [February] 1836, rumors flew about that Santa Anna and his Mexican troops were on the way to San Antonio. There was no way to trace these reports to any authentic source. But their very persistency gave rise to suspicion and credence in the minds of the brave Texans.

As a consequence, Travis, who was at that time in command of the troops at the Alamo, sent out scouts who were to locate the Mexicans under Santa Anna, if possible, and to bring in accurate information as to their whereabouts, and their probable destination. If it were possible, the scouts were to bring in an estimate of the probable force of the Mexican troops, so that action might be taken in accordance with the information so secured.

There is living today a descendant of one of these scouts, from whom this information has been secured. Some of it sheds a new light on the situation that finally culminated in the massacre in the historic little mission on the plaza in San Antonio.

Police Captain Andres Coy is the son of one of the messengers sent out by Colonel Travis.

Intelligence Needed.

According to the story told to Captain Coy by his father, the command under Colonel Travis believed that they were unable to withstand a concerted attack by the Mexican army, if it were true that Santa Anna really was headed towards San Antonio.

Plans were being discussed as to the advisability of resisting the attack or moving out of San Antonio for the purpose of augmenting the forces available for actual fighting. There was considerable discussion, until finally Davy Crockett, who wanted to be right before he went ahead, proposed a plan.

"If it is true that Santa Anna is coming to San Antonio," he said, "then our plans must be made one way. If he is not coming to San Antonio, they must be made another way. The proper thing to do is to find out whether he is coming to San Antonio. Isn't that so? Well, let's send out men to find out where he is and what he intends to do."

The suggestion met with instant approval from Travis and from Bowie, who was listening to the conversation from his cot in the next room, where he lay ill. So it was decided to send out a reconnaissance party to locate the army of Mexicans under Santa Anna and to discover their probable destination.

Goes on Reconnaissance.

Among the men sent on this errand was Trinidad Coy, father of the present police captain. He mounted his horse and faced to the south, in an attempt to follow the trail of rumor that led from San Antonio back to the Mexican forces.

As he proceeded on his way the scent grew warmer. Day by day he became convinced that there was truth in the rumor, that Santa Anna was on his way to the city of San Antonio. Several times he was sent off on a cold trail — he traveled roads that led him farther and farther from his quest. Then he would retrace his way and pick up the trail where he had left it.

He was without news from home. Days had passed now and he was without the least intimation that would lead him to believe that he should continue his quest. By day he would ride and ride, stopping now and then to inquire the latest news of a farmer or to verify a report that had come to him further up the road. Sometimes he passed hours without seeing a human being. Then, when he had stopped for the night and was rolling a cigarette at the home of some lone farmer, or when the coals of his campfire glowed brightly in the clear nights, he would begin to wonder whether, after all, he had better not give up the search and return to San Antonio.

In a Quandary.

Coy was a brave man. He knew that Travis' forces were inadequate to withstand any attack from a great force. He knew the tremendous importance of the coming battles and realized the need Travis had of every possible rifleman.

The thought distressed him. He was not of the calibre that

prefers to be a spectator of events. His was the tribe that chose rather to do, when there was need of men of action. The problem was a hard one.

If Travis had need of him in San Antonio, if one of the other men had arrived with news of the actual approach of the Mexican troops, then his place was in San Antonio. And without loss of time he would present himself before his commander, prepared to take whatever orders the commander might choose to give.

If, though, none of the other men had been able to obtain news of the invaders, and if Coy was on the track of real news of such importance, it was his plain duty to work out his string to the end and to come back with the news that these men so anxiously awaited.

There were no telegraphs in those days in Texas. News could reach him from Colonel Travis only by means of another messenger. If there was no danger of an attack by Santa Anna's army, there would be no need to send word to Coy. If there were danger of such an attack the garrison could not afford to send a messenger. For one able to deliver such a message was able to bear a gun in the fight for independence.

So Coy knew he would not hear from Travis. He knew his orders and they were plain and distinct. He was to find the Mexican army and report its strength, its whereabouts and its probable destination to Travis. That was all. If he performed this task and ill came of it, the fault was surely not his.

Great News Comes.

But this staunch old fighter did not view the matter in this light. If there was going to be fighting and he was needed, he was going to be present. He determined to spend three more days in the search and then retrace his steps, unless he had some urgent reason to continue on his way.

For two days there was the same story of conflicting information. Farmers along the road had heard that the Mexicans were approaching. They had been hearing this for some weeks. They had no authentic information. They had merely heard the rumor when they met other men on the road at the little market towns. No one positively knew anything. Coy became disheartened. He decided to return. He made plans to go to San Antonio the next day.

Then, while the men were smoking silently after supper, a neighbor came in with great news. The Mexcians were close by. They had made camp for the night only a few miles down the road.

They were on their way to San Antonio. At last the fact was assured.

Coy called the farmer's son to him and ordered that his horse be saddled at once. Cautioning his friends not to disclose the fact of his presence or his mission he mounted and started to ride away. His horse was unwilling. Here was a new and astonishing difficulty. The sturdy cow pony that had never failed him in any emergency now refused to move. While Coy was pondering the situation the horse sank to his knees and lay down.

Loco Weed.

"He has been eating somethin," said Coy. Turning to the farmer's boy, he inquired, "What have you given my horse?"

"Nothing," answered the boy.

"But you did," insisted Coy. "What was it?"

"Nothing," repeated the boy. "I just turned him into the corral to graze and threw him some hay."

The farmer spoke up. "Into which corral did you turn him? The big one?"

"Yes, sir."

"Fool! Did you not know that you had thrown there all the loco weed that came in from the wagons today?"

The boy hung his head. "I forgot," he said.

While the boy went for one of the farmer's horses to take the place of the sick animal the father explained that he had sent wagons out into fields that day to gather grasses and hay for fodder and that much of the dreaded loco weed had been found among it. The dangerous weed had been separated and thrown into the big corral, where the animals could not get to it. While he was apologizing for the boy's carelessness, the youngster came back leading a wiry little pony. Coy appraised the animal's strength and stamina. Then, apparently satisfied, he mounted and sped on his way to give the warning.

Now, if ever, he must be sure. Now, if ever, must his speed

be great, his caution true, his judgement certain. The fate of Texas hung on his hands. Could he reach the mission in San Antonio in time? He whipped up his horse to a swifter gallop.

Discovered.

"Halt!"

The word rang out in the night like a pistol shot. Voices followed it and Coy recognized the Mexican accent. These must be scouts or outposts of Santa Anna's army. He dug the spurs into his horse and flew down the road.

"Halt!"

Again the command stung the ears of the flying Texan. He only pressed forward the harder. Behind him on the road he heard the patter of many hoofs in hard pursuit.

Oh, for the little trusty pony now, whose feet were so true, whose chest so deep, whose endurance untiring. Hard, indeed, the fate that caused him to become poisoned on such a night! Then, with horror, Coy noticed that his horse was failing him. Its head sagged, its steps were staggering and blind. He whipped it up, he drove the cruel spurs deep into the quivering side. The horse threw up its head and with a last gasp of speed, jumped forward a pace or two and fell forward — dead.

The pursuers were hard behind him. Coy dodged into the brush. He heard the soldiers stop in the road where had fallen his horse, heard the quick command to scatter and find him in the brush. He crawled on his hands and knees away from his pursuers. Then, from nowhere, a Mexican soldier jumped upon his back and called for help. In another moment he was a prisoner.

Called before the commander of the little troop, he explained that he was on his way to a neighboring little town to see a sick sister, that he was in no way connected with the Texas army, that all he desired was permission to depart unmolested.

The Mexican commandant pondered awhile. "Well," he decided, "you may be telling the truth. But I believe that you ate some of the loco weed that you fed to your horse there in the road. You come with us."

Too Late.

They carried him back to the main army. With them, as a prisoner, he was taken to San Antonio. One day they appeared before the city. Coy afterwards learned that their appearance was entirely unexpected. The defenders were taken by surprise.

He was kept in the Mexican camp while preparations were made to attack the band of faithful heroes in the little church. With great avidity he saw the work go forward that was to destroy his comrades to whom he should have brought word. He cursed the luck that had tied his hands in this important of all important hours. The preparations of warfare went on. The attack commenced. With unholy joy he saw the Mexican troops beaten back, only to surge forward again, overpowering the brave defenders by sheer weight of numbers. He longed to join his friends.

Looking hastily about him he saw that the camp was deserted. All the hangers-on had followed the line of soldiery. He worked his bonds against a stone until they parted. He made his way out of the camp, followed a well-known path that led around the city and in another hour he had arrived at a point in back of the chapel of the Alamo, from where he could join his comrades.

Only a bank of cottonwood trees hid them from his view. He forced his way through the underbrush. The Alamo lay before him. There were no signs of fighting. All was quiet. Only, before his eyes, there rose the heavy black cloud from a smoking pile.

It was the funeral pyre of his friends.[43]

SUSANNA DICKINSON

Messenger of Defeat

Oral evidence for this story was presented by Paul Griffith, a great-great-grandson of Alamo survivor Susanna Dickinson.

Weary with exhaustion and numb from the horror she had

witnessed, Susanna Dickinson stumbled with her baby toward the house. Darkness had already fallen on the prairie, making it difficult for her to see. Rocks tripped her and patches of brush scraped her legs.

Susanna didn't seem to notice or care, though. All she saw was the house. A cry for help finally broke the tranquility of the night.

Inside the house, John Bruno and his wife, Sarah, awoke to Dickinson's cry. The couple lived alone near some woods outside of Gonzales, and they were alarmed by the strange voice.

John cautiously went to the front door with his rifle. He called out, squinting into the darkness.

Susanna, with her dress shredded and her face blackened with dirt, emerged from the dark holding her fifteen-month-old baby girl, Angelina. John was shocked.

The man quickly escorted Susanna and her baby into the house, discovering she had been accompanied by a Negro slave named Joe. Dickinson told John the slave was hiding in the nearby woods.

Sarah immediately took measures to comfort the obviously distraught woman and her child, covering them with a blanket to help keep them warm. The icy night air had given them both the chills.

The Brunos huddled near the woman and attempted to calm her nerves. Still puzzled, the couple asked her what had happened.

Tears welled in Susanna Dickinson's eyes. She looked up, still cradling her little girl, and began to sob. Words and tears flowed simultaneously in the minutes which followed as she recounted the horrifying scene at Bexar. The Brunos listened intently to a tale they would never forget.

Besieged by thousands of Mexican soldiers, the Texians defiantly stood their ground. They fought to the last man, including her husband, Almeron, Susanna would say over and over. She would retell the fateful end on numerous occasions throughout her lifetime: None of the defenders survived.

Yet the Brunos would be the first to hear of the legendary fall of the Alamo . . .[44]

*   *   *

Photo of Susanna Dickinson
from Daughters of the Republic of Texas Library.

Events leading to the bloody March 6 battle came fast and furious for the pioneering Tennessee woman.

On February 23, Mexican General Santa Anna came within sight of Bexar with his troops. Some *Tejanos* scurried from the streets, while others sought refuge in the Alamo.

Almeron galloped to the Don Ramon Musquiz household, where he and Susanna were boarding a number of Americans. Among them were Dr. John Sutherland and the former congressman and noted frontiersman David Crockett.

Almeron quickly ordered his wife, "Give me the baby, jump up behind me, and ask no questions."[45] Susanna said they were soon within the walls of the old, crumbling mission fortress.

A great number of civilians moved about the Alamo compound, but when faced with the dangers of staying, many fled. Susanna refused to join the exodus. She chose to remain with her husband during this perilous hour.[46]

The siege began shortly after her decision.

For the next eleven days, Susanna chipped in wherever she could. She washed the clothes of some defenders, including the fine gentleman's attire belonging to Crockett. Susanna, like her peers, greatly enjoyed the company of Colonel Crockett. He was quite amiable, and on several occasions would engage in a musical concert of sorts to help lift the spirits of the men.

Crockett would play the fiddle and Scotsman John McGregor would play his bagpipes. The two would match notes to the great amusement of those around them whenever there was a lull in the fighting.

Charming moments such as those were few and far between within the walls of the Alamo.

Susanna told how each defender made a life-or-death decision when Lieutenant Colonel Travis drew a line in the dirt with his sword.

"My soldiers, I am going to meet the fate that becomes me. Those who will stand by me, let them remain, but those who desire to go, let them go and who crosses the line that I have drawn, shall go!"[47]

Only one defender chose to step out of the ranks, a man named Moses Rose.

The man was gone the next day.

As the final battle drew closer, Almeron moved his wife and

child into the Alamo chapel, where the thick limestone walls seemed to offer a safer haven. Susanna spent countless hours in one of the chapel's cold, dark rooms listening to the boom of cannon and the crack of rifles.

In the early morning hours of March 6, Susanna was awakened by the roar of cannon. The darkened chapel walls shook.

The frightened woman squeezed her baby. Around little Angelina's neck hung a heavy, gold ring with a black cat's eye stone on a string. The ring had been given to her by Travis. The lieutenant colonel knew he wouldn't need the ring once the heavy assaults began.

Sadly, Susanna often recalled, he was right.

Moments later, Almeron burst into the room.

"Great God, Sue, the Mexicans are within our walls! All is lost! If they spare you, save my child!"[48]

Almeron then gave his wife a parting kiss and darted from the chapel sanctuary, whaling away at his Mexican assailants with the barrel of his gun. Susanna would never see her husband again.[49]

Desperate scenes sped before her eyes at a furious pace.

Several defenders appeared before Susanna during the final assault, including a Gonzales boy named Galba Fuqua. The sixteen-year-old Fuqua found Susanna in the chapel and tried to tell her something, perhaps to carry a message to his family. Blood flowed from Fuqua's mouth as he held his jaw together with his hands. He could not speak. The boy could only give her an agonizing gaze before bolting from the room, ultimately to his death.

Three unarmed gunners who abandoned their then-useless guns soon followed.

Volunteer Anthony Wolfe begged for mercy, Susanna recalled, and was instantly killed.

Jacob Walker, a scrappy artilleryman from Nacogdoches, bolted into the room next, pursued by four Mexican soldiers. Walker was pierced with a number of bayonets, hoisted overhead like a "bundle of fodder," and shot.

Susanna then saw Maj. Robert Evans make a heroic effort to reach the magazine room with a torch in hand. If all was lost, it was generally known throughout the garrison, one of the defenders would blow up the ammunition supply.

Evans was carrying out that order, but Mexican bullets reached him first.

Sporadic gunfire sounded even after the two-hour struggle. Susanna, along with other women and children, fearfully huddled against the wall in one of the chapel rooms. A Mexican officer suddenly appeared in the doorway and bellowed, "Is Mrs. Dickinson here?"

"Yes," Susanna replied.

"If you wish to save yourself," the man said, "follow me."

Susanna slowly rose, pressing Angelina tightly against her chest. She followed the Mexican officer out of the chapel, now stained with blood, and was horrified by the sights around the Alamo compound.

Lying everywhere were the dead and dying. She struggled to step around and over them, only to hear the faint groans of those now destined to die.

Susanna pressed on, gazing for a moment at Crockett's mutilated body which lay "between the church and the two-story barracks building, his peculiar cap by his side."

Moments later, a gunshot pierced a thigh.[50] A Mexican soldier carried her to the Musquiz house, where she was treated and held with the other women and children of the Alamo for the night.

Santa Anna hastily questioned each the next morning. For Susanna, who along with her baby was the lone Anglo survivor, the Mexican general had special instructions. He handed her a letter to give to the Texian rebels.

The letter's message said that anyone who resisted Mexican rule would meet the same fate as those in the Alamo.

Santa Anna then placed Susanna and her baby on a mule and ordered three Mexican guards to escort her to the third picket line. From there, she was instructed to follow the "beef" trail toward Gonzales until she came to the first house.

Little did John and Sarah Bruno know that the first house would be theirs and that they would play host to the messenger of the Alamo.[51]

PART III

Out of the Ashes

General Santa Anna gazed over the blackened and mangled corpses inside the Alamo. Greeting Capt. Fernando Urriza, His Excellency said with a shrug, "It was but a small affair."[1]

Santa Anna soon ordered the bodies of the Texians burned.

A company of dragoons was sent with Francisco Antonio Ruiz, *alcalde* to Bexar, to gather wood from the neighboring forest. The dead Texians were then laid between layers of wood, until all the defenders were cleared from the compound.

Kindling was placed throughout the pile, and at about 5:00 P.M., the fire was started.

Smoke billowed skyward as the funeral pyre took on an eerie sight. The bodies of the defenders were eventually reduced to ashes.[2]

The battle was over.

For the Mexican victors, however, the battle was merely beginning. Taking the Alamo was a costly venture. The Mexicans lost more than some of their best fighting men. They also lost any psychological edge they may have possessed.

If the unfortunate massacre wasn't demoralizing enough to the Mexicans, the vengeance in the eyes of Texians would be.

The Texians would indeed remember the Alamo.

The struggle was also just beginning for the widows and orphans of Alamo defenders. News of the slaughter sparked a mass exodus to the safer eastern settlements. The exodus became known as the "Runaway Scrape."

In many ways, these women and children displayed as much courage during the retreat as those who died within the walls of the Alamo.

117

GEORGE C. KIMBLE

Final Farewell

Oral evidence for the following story was presented by Linda Halliburton, a great-great-great-great-granddaughter of Alamo defender George C. Kimble. As a child she heard stories about her Alamo ancestor from her great-grandmother, Rhoda Elizabeth Kimble Hurt.

The gentle flow of the creek water provided a peaceful atmosphere for Prudence Nash Kimble that cold February afternoon in 1836. She was washing clothes in the icy water as her two-year-old son, Charles Chester, scurried around at her feet.

A few moments later, the serenity would be dashed away.

George C. Kimble, Prudence's husband, would give her news as sad as death. He walked down to the creek, looked his pregnant wife in the eyes, and told her he was going to the aid of the men at the Alamo. Mexican forces had encircled them; their situation was desperate.

"Prudence," he said, "I probably won't return."

With that, Kimble rode out of Prudence's life and into history.

Kimble was a man of great size and strength. His son, Charles, grew to be a lean and muscular six-foot-two, 200-pounder. George was said to be even bigger.

Kimble's life had changed drastically since he left New York a bachelor. He moved to Texas to cash in on the Mexican land grants, and ended up starting a family.

At thirty-three Kimble married Prudence, a pretty widow, on June 26, 1832. Soon after, they had Charles. Another child was on the way.

Mexico granted Kimble 420 acres at Green DeWitt's colony, but he opted to live near the promising town of Gonzales on his wife's property from her previous marriage. In Gonzales, on Water Street, he owned a prosperous hat factory with Almeron Dickinson, who was already trapped inside the Alamo with his wife, Susanna.

Charles Kimble, son of Alamo defender George Kimble. He was two years old when his father rode to the Alamo. He was said to have closely resembled his father.

— Photo courtesy of Linda Halliburton

Kimble was the commanding officer of the Gonzales Ranging Company of Mounted Volunteers, and as lieutenant, he knew his place was at the Alamo in Bexar. On February 27 he picked up fifty-two pounds of coffee from Stephen Smith as part of supplies for "the relief of the boys at Bexar." He then rode to Bexar with Capt. Albert Martin, John W. Smith, George Cottle, and twenty-eight other volunteers from Gonzales. The daring group cut through the enemy lines and arrived at the Alamo on March 1 around 3:00 A.M. in the pouring rain.

A thunderous cheer from the defenders greeted their arrival.

Kimble's mind was obviously on his family.

Back near Gonzales, Prudence awaited word. She received her answer shortly after March 6 when a messenger brought the tragic news of the Alamo: Her husband and the rest of the defenders were slaughtered by Mexican troops. Mexican forces were now heading east.

Prudence hardly cracked. She was used to tough times. After all, her first husband had died of an accidental shooting in Gonzales. Time to mourn would come later.

Saving her family was now top priority. She loaded Charles, the three children from her previous marriage, and everything the family owned in a wagon. They fled with other Texas emigrants toward Louisiana.

In June, while still on the wagon in the prairie, Prudence gave birth to twin girls — Jane and Amanda. Both survived, and so did Prudence. But survival wouldn't come easy for the widowed mother of six.

A burned homestead greeted her upon her return. Mexican General Santa Anna and his troops had scorched everything in their path as they roared through Gonzales. All livestock had been slaughtered.

The only thing left at the Kimble homestead was a hen sitting on a nest of eggs on what remained of the porch. The hen had a broken leg.[3]

JOHN W. SMITH

Deathly Silence

Cordella Truesdell presented the oral evidence for the following story. Truesdell is a great-great-granddaughter of Alamo courier John W. Smith.

John William Smith and his band of twenty-five volunteers slowly crept toward the Alamo. After two days of hard riding from Gonzales, the men were getting closer. And now it was time to proceed with caution.

Thousands of Mexican troops under General Santa Anna had encircled the Alamo, Smith told his volunteers. Patrols were everywhere.

Smith was leery of the fact that he didn't hear any cannon or gunfire. Lieutenant Colonel Travis had told Smith he would fire a cannon each day as a signal when Smith left the Alamo as a courier March 3. Silence filled the air.

Smith ordered a halt for the night at Cibolo, near what is today Sutherland Springs. Eight scouts were sent west toward Bexar the next morning to gain more information.

Waiting was hard for Smith. He knew the situation was desperate for his friends and neighbors trapped in the Alamo. He quickly grew restless.

The garrison was being manned by some 180 men the night he left. Two days earlier, on March 1, he and Dr. John Sutherland helped thirty-two volunteers from Gonzales slip through the Mexican lines and into the Alamo. Spirits were boosted that day.

Smith just hoped he wasn't too late.

Still, all he heard was silence.

John W. Smith, at forty-four, had poured his heart and soul into the fight for independence, though a year earlier he was a member of the Peace Party. How times had changed. He became convinced Santa Anna intended to wipe out the Anglo settlers in Texas. Independence from Mexico, he came to realize, was the only true answer.

Smith's home in Bexar soon evolved into an underground headquarters for the War Party. Samuel A. Maverick, a signer of the Texas Declaration of Independence, joined the household in September of 1835, and the movement continued to gain momentum.

Their activities became so notorious that Mexican Col. Domingo de Ugartechea placed Smith and his family under house arrest on October 16, 1835. None of the Mexican soldiers knew that Smith spoke fluent Spanish. Four years earlier he had married Maria de Jesus Curbelo, who came from one of the prominent old Canary Island families.

Smith thus spent his imprisonment carefully listening to the plans of the Mexican authorities. He saw their strengths and heard about their weaknesses. Supplies were low, as was morale.

Imprisoned Erastus "Deaf" Smith, Maverick, and Smith repaid the Mexicans on December 1 when they escaped Bexar and rejoined the Texian Army a day later. Smith promptly drew up a map of the Mexican defenses, and along with Maverick and the savvy "Deaf" Smith, urged an immediate attack on the town.

They knew the Mexicans were vulnerable.

On December 5, Smith and fellow scouts Hendrick Arnold, "Deaf" Smith, and Maverick guided the attacking Texian columns into Bexar. The fury was unleashed as the savage fight went house-to-house.

Five days later, on December 10, Gen. Martin Perfecto de Cos raised the white flag of surrender. The Alamo was in Texian hands. But the battle had just begun.

Smith worked at the Alamo as a storekeeper for the Texian Army until February 23, when Travis called on him for an urgent mission. The lieutenant colonel ordered Smith and Sutherland to scout for the advancing army of Santa Anna.

They soon returned with alarming news. Santa Anna was a mere two miles west of Bexar.

Travis immediately sent the two reliable scouts to Gonzales with some of his last lines of communication and another plea for help.

Now Smith was killing time on the prairie with a fresh group of recruits, waiting word from his scouts. Had the Alamo fallen? Why was the countryside so silent?

Smith grew impatient.

Suddenly, his eight scouts rode up. The advance guard of the Mexican cavalry forced them to hastily retreat. The Mexicans were only eight miles west of the Cibolo.

Their worst fears were confirmed. The Alamo must have fallen.

Smith and his men quickly mounted their horses and sped for Gonzales to warn the citizens. Their arrival confirmed the news brought by *Tejanos* Anselmo Borgara and Andres Barcena of the Alamo's defeat.

The Runaway Scrape was on.

For the next several days, while on the run, Smith engaged in his most disturbing duty thus far. He worked with Gail Borden and Gerald Navan to compile the names of those he believed died at the Alamo.

The list was first published in the *Telegraph and Texas Register* on March 24, and the silence was shattered.[4]

GORDON C. JENNINGS

Little Katie's Ride

Lee Spencer presented the oral evidence for the following story. Spencer, who has gathered various family legends over the years, is a great-great-great-great-granddaughter of Alamo artilleryman Gordon C. Jennings.

Pigtailed Katie Jennings was just ten years old when her mother, Catherine, hoisted her onto the family's best horse in March of 1836. Little did the youngster know she would become the Paul Revere of the Texas Revolution.

Catherine had just learned that the Mexican Army, led by dictator Santa Anna, had captured the Alamo. She wondered if her husband, Gordon C. Jennings, had survived the battle. He had joined the Alamo garrison shortly before the December 11, 1835, battle at Bexar, leaving his wife and their four children behind at their cabin near the town of Bastrop.

Sketch of Gordon C. Jennings.
— Drawing by Gary Zaboly

Gordon's fate haunted her. Was he still alive? There was hope, but Catherine didn't have time to worry.

Word was out that a large division of Mexican infantry and cavalry had reached the Colorado River April 12, and the settlers believed their mission was to wipe out every man, woman, and child in their path.

Gen. Antonio Gaona led the formidable Mexican force, which largely consisted of the Morelos Permanente Infantry Battalion. The Morelos Battalion was defeated at the Battle of Bexar in December, and in the eyes of the Texians, those soldiers were breaking their parole.

Luckily for the Jennings and other families north of the Colorado River, the Mexican crossing was delayed because of flood conditions and the lack of boats. Mexican troops instead entertained themselves with looting and whiskey.

Danger still lurked, however, for the settlers in Austin's little colony. They knew the Mexicans were only a boat ride away from invading their homes.

So with Mexican troops wearing out horses to overtake anything in their way, Catherine Jennings set Katie on a bareback horse outside their cabin before joining the Runaway Scrape. Catherine gave her instructions to warn the neighbors. She told Katie to hurry and ride out with the last family she reached. They would reunite en route to Louisiana.

"No matter what," Catherine finally ordered, "don't come back here."

Katie then spurred her horse with her bare heel and galloped off. With pigtails flapping in the wind, she took one last glance back before riding off into the distant prairie.

Robert Williamson, in the meantime, evacuated Bastrop.

Williamson, known as "Three Legged Willie" because of a permanently bent right leg held up by a wooden cane, returned to Bastrop after the fall of the Alamo. He was in charge of a small company of men whose job was to protect the area from Mexicans or warring Comanches.

By this time, even General Houston was in retreat. He had already ordered Gonzales to be torched, and frightened settlers fled in his tracks for the safety of the eastern settlements.

Catherine and her family were the last of the holdouts.

They came from a hardy breed of pioneers who chose the wide-open prairie as opposed to the safer settlements near Bastrop. The land on the upper bend of the Colorado River was rich and fertile with black dirt, but was also plagued by Indian raids. The Comanche were among the most notorious visitors.

Still, for free-spirited settlers like Ed Burleson, Jesse Billingsley, Robert Coleman and Jennings, the land and adventurous way of life was worth the risk. Catherine's oldest son, Willis Avery, was among those daring few. He settled nearby on Brushy Creek.

Gordon C. Jennings was as tough as they came despite being a simple farmer from Missouri. He enjoyed his tobacco and liquor as well as his freedom. And, at fifty-seven, he was the oldest known defender in the Alamo. He eventually became a corporal in Capt. William Carey's artillery company, a position he held during the Siege of Bexar.

Billingsley organized the Mina Volunteers when word reached Bastrop on February 26 of the Alamo siege. Two days later, the new company marched to join other forming companies in Gonzales to relieve the Alamo.

Willis Avery was among the volunteers. Gordon's stepson, like family friends Burleson and Coleman, would later free Texas from the grip of the Mexican Army at the Battle of San Jacinto. Burleson would lead the 1st Infantry with ferocity in the eighteen-minute onslaught.

These were rugged men who fought for their way of life every day, and their women were no different. They, too, were blazers in the untamed western frontier of Texas.

Time after time, Catherine displayed a remarkable resilience. Her first husband, Vincent Avery, was a seafarer who had died at sea. He left her to raise their son, Willis, in North Carolina. She eventually made her way to Tennessee, where she married William McCutheon. They had two sons, but little else.

In 1818, after a stormy marriage, Catherine removed herself from the relationship. The fiery, independent Catherine left one son with McCutheon, loaded her other two boys in a wagon, and journeyed to Missouri.

There she met Gordon Jennings.

Fate sent them to Texas in 1833 and into the heat of the revolution. Like her gallant husband, who was later confirmed dead at the Alamo, Catherine played her role in Texas independence.

Survival was again her calling. With Gordon's fate unknown to her, Catherine took charge of the family. She loaded her children, Willis' pregnant wife and small daughter, and all the possessions they could carry into a wagon. They then headed toward the Colorado River.

There, on the banks of the Colorado, Catherine helped her daughter-in-law deliver a baby. But the exodus would not be stopped by the new arrival. The Jennings clan continued east on the Gosher Cut across the open prairie toward San Felipe de Austin to join the northern end of the Runaway Scrape.

Somewhere south of present-day Warrenton in Fayette County, the Bastrop refugees turned north on the old La Bahia Road and trekked toward Washington-on-the-Brazos. By the time they arrived, the community was nearly abandoned since the interim government adjourned March 17. Once across the Brazos, their journey became bogged down by the nasty, wet weather. Soon it would take a full day to travel four miles.

Young John Holland Jenkins, whose mother was widowed from the Alamo battle, was among those dispatched by Burleson from the main army to help evacuate the families. He later recalled, "It was pitiful and distressing to behold the extremity of the families, as sometimes a team would bog down, and women with their babies in their arms, surrounded by little children, had to wade almost waist deep in places."[5]

Catherine was among the courageous.

Eventually, her caravan reached Robbins Ferry at the junction of the La Bahia and Old San Antonio roads. In front of them were dozens of families camped on the banks of the Trinity River. The refugees nervously waited for their turn to cross, each wondering about the proximity of the onrushing Mexican troops.

Heavy rains swelled the Trinity River five miles wide, and one small ferry worked nonstop to cross all who waited. Catherine waited a week for her family's turn.

The storming Mexican troops were on her mind, but foremost in her thoughts was the fate of Gordon and little Katie.

Even little Katie shared in the courageous spirit of her parents. Years later, she would recount her fascinating life.

Katie would tell of how she received the scars on her body while escaping an Indian attack in 1842. The chilling account started on Christmas morning shortly after she and her first husband, Casper Whisler, homesteaded in Collin County with two other families.

Casper and another man were cutting logs for a cabin when they were ambushed by Indians. Casper was immediately shot dead.

The gunshots and screams instantly told Katie what was happening. She ducked into some thick brush to cover her tracks while she made her way to the main creek. From there, she submerged herself in water up to her head and hid behind some driftwood. Twenty yards away, she watched an Indian steal her husband's horse.

Katie, after watching the Indians leave, made her escape through briars and dense thicket. She arrived at the settlement of Throckmorton later that night, her clothes tattered and nearly gone.

But as dramatic as the story was, Katie's tales always went back to the Texas Revolution and the spring of 1836. She would tell of her father's death at the Alamo, of her family's struggle for survival in the Runaway Scrape and of her heart-pounding ride.

Today, descendants still boast about little Katie's ride. And why not? On that day, family honor soared to new heights as another hero of the Texas Revolution emerged.[6]

JAMES GEORGE

Buck Up and Kick In

Janelle Sewell presented the oral evidence for the following story. Sewell is a great-great-great-granddaughter of Alamo defender James George.

Thirty-two men rode for Bexar in early 1836, stirred with patriotism and emotion. A small band of friends, neighbors, and fellow countrymen were surrounded by vast forces of the Mexican Army at the Alamo garrison, and their dramatic appeal for help touched every heart in the town of Gonzales.

As a group, the thirty-two men were known as the Gonzales Ranging Company of Mounted Volunteers. Alone, they were farmers, cattlemen, and businessmen. They were common folk engaged in an uncommon act.

Among the brave was Jesse McCoy, the town sheriff. There was Isaac Millsaps, who left his blind wife and seven children behind to answer the call of war. And there was George W. Tumlinson, a wayward twenty-two-year-old who came from a family of fighters.

Each had his own reasons for riding into danger, supplying his own horse, firearm, and ammunition to boot. Yet each could find common ground in his defiance of the Mexican government. Mexico, they believed, was taking away rights already granted to them.

James William George was among those who wished to buck up and kick in.

Like his companions, George had his own reasons for joining the Gonzales relief force. He wanted to protect what he and his family desperately sacrificed to obtain — a new start in life.

George first heard of the vast prairies and abundance of free land in Texas while living in Fayetteville, Tennessee. Word spread throughout the community about a man named Green DeWitt who had established a colony in the Mexican province of Tejas. George and his wife, Elizabeth, entertained the notion of a new start in a foreign land.

So struck by the idea was George, he set out on his own for Texas in 1829 to scout the land. He returned to Fayetteville with news of the perfect location, a plot of land near Plum Creek, some fourteen miles east of Gonzales.

The Georges were soon packed and trekking to Texas along with other DeWitt Colony recruits. Among the Tennessee pioneers who joined the Georges on the trip to Texas was blacksmith Almeron Dickinson, who lived in nearby Hardeman County.

George and his family reached Gonzales on February 20, 1831. Their migration had taken them down the Mississippi River into Missouri, through Arkansas and through Nacogdoches, Texas, along the Trammell Trace. From there, the family followed the Old Spanish Road into Gonzales. Their reward for the arduous journey was a league of land.

William Dearduff, Elizabeth's brother, would soon join them in Texas to share in the dream. He received a quarter league of land because of his status as a bachelor.

George and Dearduff built the family's first Texas home from split oak logs near Plum Creek. The cabin had a dogtrot and fireplaces. From that humble beginning, George established himself as a farmer and cattleman.

Now George was faced with enduring Mexican rule or fleeing all he had built for himself and his family. Neither option was to his liking.

George would instead choose to fight.

Naturally, the decision was not easy. In standing up for what he believed, George left behind all that he loved. Saying goodbye to his wife, a 100-pound, red-haired fireball of Dutch descent, was especially hard. So was leaving behind his five children, Mary Jane, Margaret, Rachel, James Joseph, and Matilda.

But George knew the fight was for them too.

Still, George wanted to ensure his family's safety as much as possible. He called down the lane to his farmhand, John A. Rowe, for help.

Rowe, a crippled bootmaker, was a bachelor neighbor who worked at times for board at the George farm. He was asked by George to watch over his family during his absence, and in exchange, would be provided his keep. Rowe accepted the offer.

George and Dearduff then turned their horses toward Gonzales and their attention toward the looming battle in Bexar. Neither man knew for certain what lay ahead, but each was ready to embrace his fate.

The moment of truth for the volunteers came during the early-morning hours of March 1 as they slowly crept toward the Alamo. Darkness engulfed the group as they moved closer and closer to enemy lines. Suddenly, in the stillness of the cold morning air, the company made a dash for the mission fortress.

Gunfire erupted in the confusion as Mexican soldiers scrambled to pick off the daring volunteers. Alamo defenders fired back once they realized those rushing forward were friends, not foes.

The element of surprise worked. All thirty-two members of the Gonzales Ranging Company made it safely through the gates of the Alamo, where they were greeted with handshakes and cheers. Dickinson was one of those who gratefully greeted George.

Immortality would soon follow.

On March 6, George, Dearduff, and the rest of the Alamo defenders were killed by superior numbers of Mexican soldiers. A huge funeral pyre would prove to be a lasting impression for those who would hear of their grand sacrifice.

Elizabeth, meanwhile, carried on the George name in the Runaway Scrape.

She joined General Houston, who camped across the road from the George farm, in the rush for the Sabine River. She loaded up the family's cart and took along some cows so they would have milk and butter for the journey.

When Elizabeth's daughters, Mary and Rachel, grew tired of riding, they decided to walk despite the constant rain and flooding. Margaret drove the cows. At one point, Mary and Rachel became mired in mud. Luckily for them, two men on horseback spotted them and returned them to the family cart. The two little girls weren't even missed in all the confusion.

The Georges' tragedy ended nearly a year later upon their return to Plum Creek. Like many others, their home had been burned and their cattle had been run off. Most disturbing of all to the family was the absence of their father and uncle.

In their place, however, was freedom.[7]

SAMPSON CONNELL

Alamo Wagon Master

Oral evidence for this story was presented by Pat Cloud, a great-great-great-granddaughter of Alamo wagon master Sampson Connell.

Sampson Connell's wagon rambled through the main entrance to the Alamo one February day. Aboard was Connell's fourteen-year-old son, who also was named by Sampson, and some badly needed supplies for the garrison.

Lt. Col. James C. Neill was in charge of the Alamo troops at the time, and Connell was soon included on the latest muster roll. Connell was an ancient warrior whose time in battle dated back to Andrew Jackson's legendary victory at New Orleans.

Connell climbed aboard his wagon when the time arrived and he journeyed to his next assignment. Shortly afterward, the Mexican Army laid siege to San Antonio de Bexar and the Alamo. Connell's delivery was the last for the garrison's defenders.

The Bastrop native would later play a role at the Battle of San Jacinto, where he worked as a wagon master. Another of his sons, sixteen-year-old David Cook, also took part in the famous fight which ultimately won Texas independence.

Connell's other children shared in the danger of the times. Since Connell was widowed in 1834, his eldest daughter, Elizabeth, became head of the household in Bastrop. Siblings William, James, George, and Mary Ann intently listened to Elizabeth when they heard the news of the advancing Mexican Army. The Alamo had fallen and the Mexicans were coming.

David Cook Connell's future wife, Sarah Jane Clark, would also encounter the danger of the revolution. Sarah was a nine-year-old at the time of the Alamo's fall. She was living with her mother, Mary Brisbin Clark Deleplain, and her stepfather, Absalom C. Deleplain, when news of the Alamo slaughter reached their Mina home.

The family quickly buried its silver under a washpot, ran off the livestock into the woods, loaded a cart, and fled to the east.

They later returned to find their house ravaged. Mattresses were bayoneted and feathers were everywhere. Various items were scattered about the yard and even in the trees. The livestock was nowhere to be found.

Only one thing remained — the buried silver.[8]

ISAAC MILLSAPS

Realities of War

The following story is based on Nettie Milsaps Gormanous' "The Milsaps Family, Patriotic, Hard Working, God Loving Americans." Gormanous is a great-great-granddaughter of Alamo defender Isaac Millsaps.

War cut deep in the heart of Mary Millsaps. She lost a husband and a future in one fell swoop on March 6, 1836.

Millsaps, a blind mother of seven, anxiously awaited the news of the Alamo garrison from some seventy miles away in Gonzales. Her husband, Isaac, was one of the thirty-two men from Gonzales who rode to the aid of the besieged Alamo defenders. He was a rifleman for the Gonzales Ranging Company of Mounted Volunteers, and no stranger to war.

The forty-one-year-old Isaac had fought in the War of 1812 as a private in the East Tennessee Militia. He was seventeen years old at the time.[9]

Isaac was always willing to help where there was trouble. So he entered the Alamo on March 1 along with his Gonzales comrades in a daring ride through enemy lines.

Isaac's life was snuffed out, however, in the early-morning hours of March 6 when the Mexican Army massacred the entire Alamo garrison.

News of the Alamo's fall slowly reached Gonzales, and when it finally did, the horrific story set off a panic. Citizens scrambled to gather what belongings they could carry and made a mass exodus to the east.

General Houston led the retreat with his rag-tag Texian Army and its few supplies.

In the confusion, Mary Millsaps and her seven children were left behind.

When General Houston realized his blunder, he sent one of his soldiers back to Gonzales to rescue them. Mary was found waiting patiently with her children, hidden in brush along the river.[10]

Survival would be especially tough for blind Mary. She was left to raise seven children by herself, and as she discovered in the coming years, not even the Republic of Texas would help.

On May 9, 1838, Mary submitted an impassioned plea to the Republic of Texas:

> To the Honorable member of the Senate and House of Representatives of the Republic of Texas in Congress assembled. Your petitioner the under signed begs leave to represent that she is the widow of Isaac Millsaps who fell in the Alamo on the 6th of March 1836. While fighting under the command of the gallant Travis. that in March 1835 he had made application for lands in Austin's Colony which will be seen by reference to the books of that colony now in the general land office that about that time he selected and settled upon a League of land on the head waters of Labaca where he with his family resided when he was called to the defense of his country and where thet were when they heard of the retreat of Houston and the advance of the Mexican forces My self-blind and seven small children were not allowed one hour to prepare and no means of transportation we left all behind were thrown upon the world helpless and destitute in this situation. I have been struggling for 2 years and not able to return to the place we left. The prayer of your petitioner is that you pay an act to secure to me and my children land selected by my husband as I am informed that a man by the name of Jujac Roberson is making surveys that will interfere with my rights.
>
> Mary Millsaps[11]

The Republic of Texas granted a pension to Mary of $200 annually for ten years with $100 in advance on November 21, 1838.[12]

Taxes had mounted on Mary's 4,605.5 acres in Jackson County, however, because of her poor financial situation. She had accumulated a debt of $143.21, and applied for $300 owed to her from Isaac's death.

On March 3, 1840 — almost four years to the day of Isaac's fateful entrance into the Alamo — Mary's land was put up for public auction. It was sold for $115 to James A. Sylvester of Jackson County.

On December 9, 1840, Mary received the $300 from the state.[13]

CARDENAS

Conscripted Soldado

Henry Cardenas presented the oral evidence for the following story. Cardenas grew up hearing a story about his great-grandfather, who fought with Santa Anna at the Battle of the Alamo. Cardenas heard this story from his father, Enrique Trevino Cardenas, but through the years, the first name of the Mexican soldado *has been forgotten.*

Life in Saltillo was simple until the day General Santa Anna rolled through the Mexican town with his army. Santa Anna was searching for recruits on this winter day in 1836 to take north with him into the Mexican province of *Tejas*.

A revolution had already taken hold in *Tejas*, and Santa Anna planned to terminate the rebellion with one mighty sweep through the territory.

Santa Anna ordered the recruitment of the most promising males over the age of fifteen from each family in Saltillo.

For the Cardenas family, the future was at stake. The oldest of the Cardenas sons was a drunkard and a womanizer, while the younger, eighteen-year-old son was a promising young man who would someday inherit the family ranch.

The Mexican Army, naturally, selected the eighteen-year-old.

Distraught over the possibility of losing the boy in battle, the family approached the oldest son with an offer. The family offered him 500 gold pieces if he would go in place of his younger brother, which he did. Mexican Army authorities did not care. They merely wanted bodies.

The older Cardenas son then got in line with the rest of the Mexican *soldados* and began the long, grueling march toward *Tejas*.

Sketch of Cardenas fleeing Alamo after battle.
— Drawing by Gary Zaboly

Cardenas would take part in the bloody Battle of the Alamo in Bexar, where rebellious Texian forces were wiped out. Figuring the war was over, Cardenas and three companions left the army and headed back to Saltillo.

The four men eventually reached a *hacienda* near the town of Laredo. They told the man who lived there they were hungry and asked him for some food. Instead of feeding the starving *soldados*, the *ranchero* shooed them away.

Cardenas and his three companions left and hid out in some nearby brush. Once the sun set, the four men crept into the *hacienda* under the cover of darkness. They killed the family, stole their money, and took whatever food they wanted.

The *soldados* hiked back to their homes in Mexico. Cardenas returned to Saltillo 500 gold pieces richer.[14]

DOLPHIN FLOYD

A Brother's Curiosity

The following story is based on Tommie Stulting's "A Pioneer Woman and Her Family," Catherine Clark Griffin's writings, and an 1855 letter from Thomas B. Floyd to Esther Clark, the widow of Alamo defender Dolphin Floyd. Thomas was Dolphin's brother.

Stulting is a great-great-great-granddaughter of Alamo widow Esther (Berry House Floyd) Clark, while Catherine Clark Griffin was Esther's daughter.

Curiosity burned within Thomas B. Floyd for years. The last time he saw Dolphin, his brother was plowing a field. One day Dolphin left the plow in the field and headed for Texas.

But where in Texas did Dolphin go? How was he doing? Why didn't he write?

Floyd's worst intuition was realized one day when he read in a publication the names of those slain at the Alamo. Dolphin Floyd was on the list.

Still, Thomas was gripped by the unknown. There was a burning desire to know as much about his brother as possible.

What was he like in the final years of his life? Did his personality change? His habits? His morals?

Thomas lived with these questions for twenty-five years until a tip led to the whereabouts of his brother's widow in Texas. He anxiously wrote to her to satisfy his curiosity in a letter.

Georgia Troup County June 15th 1855

Dear Nephew & Sister, for such as I shall call you,

Very recently Sister Sarah Received a letter from North Carolina bearing some intelegence of our Deceased Brother Dolphin Floyd. How they got information of you and your whereabouts I cannot tell unless through the politeness of Mr. Davis Bunting. If it be the Bunting I knew in NoCa he is a man of 40 or 45 years of age. If it be the man I think he is he is well acquainted with me and all the rest of the family.

I have written two letters since 1830 to my Brother, one addressed to Orleans. That was before annexation of Texas to the States. Some time in 35 I wrote one and Directed it to Nachadoces but never received no answer & give up all hope of ever hearing from him again but always inquiring. I have given the — of my Brother to many travelers but never could get any information. I saw in some gazet of the United States but not Recollect what one; the Names of the persons of thoes that were Massacred in Texas and my Brother was one. The date of the schedule that contained the Names of the Slayn I do not recollect. I very Recollect the Name of my Broth. & David Crocket.

My Mother Received one Letter from him after he went to Texas Stating to her he was Married and had one child 18 Months old & that he Married a Widow Jones. He also wrote that he used to tell us all, while joking and talking about Marying, that he intended Marrying some old Rich widow that she might Die directly & then he would be independant. Though he had Marred, as he always had said, a Widow and that she was not very old nor very Rich. So we have never heard any more about him untill now.

Therefore I take the privilege of writing to you both Requesting you write to me as soon as these lines of my best love and Respects Reaches you and particular on the acount of my poor old aged Mother for since she has heard this much about him she is very desirous to hear more. She is now in her 86

Alamo widow Esther Clark. She was married to Dolphin Floyd when he died at the Alamo.

— Photo courtesy of Judy Deal

year & lives within 1/4 of a Mile of me with my Brother Penuel & Sister Sarah both single. So far as Respects the goods of this world they are independant. My Mother is well taken care of as Respects the comforts of this life. In fact we that are here in Georgia are all getting along well. Brother John is very Rich. I have plenty my self for my children to do well on.

Now there is one or two things I do wish to know. First I wish to know how you are situated and what your condition is Relative to living & making out in this life. Secondly what it was when you Married my Brother. Thirdly what his condition was when he Married you. Fourthly what was his reputation, whether good or bad. I wish to know whether he stood fair to the world as Respects truth and varasity & what was his general deportment. You may think I am too scrupulous & wish to know to much. My Dear Nephew & Sister, this is a great request, too much, you may think, to be revealed, but nothing less than the Revelation will satisfy me.

Now for my Reasons to wish to know them is this: to see if a person once pure as vain Mortal can be can become adulterated by leaving his county and family Circle. When He left NoCa, Novr. 22nd 1825, and took a last shake of the hand from his poor old Mother & his Brothers & Sisters, With the exception of Sin, Stain was not to be found on him. He indulged in no bad practices save that of the folly of youth. He Drank no ardent Spirits, chew no Tobaco nor used Sigrs. When he left us He made no pretentions to Religion of any sort. He was always lively and very good of company and had the good will of all that knew and was much beloved. He was very Industrous though subject to waist as we all thought.

Now I wish to know some more things. I want to know whether he was a good Husband, a kind father, a good provider & if a master a good Master neighbor, whether he was charitable, Benevolent so far as in power. I wish to know something Relative to your Birth, where you were born and of what nation. We understand you have Married since my Brother got killed to a Mr. Clark. We do not blame you for that as it is reasonably supposed that every Body tries to do the best they can. I want to know how John is getting along. It would do me so much good to hear he was doing well. We understand you had a Daughter by my Brother and she had married and since Died as her name was Elizabeth. We have two samples of Hair to be John's and Elizabeth's.

Now my Dear Sister & Nephew these Requests you may think to be Exaggerations and Spiculative. But they are the pure desiers of my heart and no speculative design in them, no farther than to know the truth.

Now if you want to know my Brothers age he was born March 6th A.D. 1804.

The times in Georgia are hard. Money is scarce. Provisions of all kind, scarce. Corn $5 per bushel, Bacon 12[1/2] cents pr. lb; Wheat has been 2 pr. Bush, Wheat Crops good. Other growing crops looks promising.

I am older than Dolphin. He was next to me. I was born Feby. 27th 1802. When he left Northcarolina we were both about one Weight, say 125 lbs. Though at this time I way 190 lbs. I am corpulent and clumsey and feel my age much. The rest of our family is all small. Brother Penuel will weigh not more than 120 and is about 45 years of age.

I have 6 living Children, 4 Sons & Two Daughters. One is dead, my oldest son. There Names are as follows.

> 1st De Witt Clinton oldest dead.
> 2nd John Curtis Elliott.
> 3rd Henry Drew.
> Thomas Penuel.
> James Dolphin.
> Rebecca Ann Priscilla.
> Martha Elizabeth Savanah.

There Mothers name was Martha Daniel Hunter. She died Octr. 14th 1840. Born Decr. 16th 1807. I Married my present wife Feby. 11th 1841, name Ann Sharp; never had but one child, stilled born.

If these lines ever Reach they leave all your connections in this county well. May they find you enjoying the same blessing is my prayr.

So I Subscribe my self your affectionate Brother and uncle untill death.

> So fare well,
> Thos B. Floyd[15]

Esther Floyd, now Esther Clark, read the letter with amazement. Memories she had tucked away for nineteen years were now as clear as yesterday. Time had eased the pain of losing Dolphin, but now she was reliving the nightmare all over again.

Suddenly, she was back in Gonzales in March of 1836.

How could she ever forget the day she heard of Dolphin's death? It was horrific. She was eight months pregnant and in the home of Mrs. Braches, along with twenty-seven other terrified wives, when news arrived of the Alamo's fall. The Mexicans gave no quarter. Every man was killed.[16]

Esther's life changed dramatically at that moment. Actually, the change had started to take place in October, when Dolphin and other citizens of Gonzales paraded the town's cannon, daring Mexican forces with a flag that read: "Come and Take It." The fight for independence had begun.

Whirlwind events soon sent Dolphin riding to Bexar with thirty-one other volunteers from Gonzales to aid those at the Alamo. Esther would never again see Dolphin.

Like many other Texas women of the time, survival didn't come easy for Esther. General Houston ordered the abandonment of Gonzales, thus sparking the Runaway Scrape. Esther loaded her most immediate necessities in a two-wheeled cart or freighter, and, along with her five children, joined the eastward movement.

One of her primary concerns on the trip was preventing the wooden axle from catching fire. Since grease was scarce, Esther kept them lubricated with her precious gourd of soft soap.[17]

Esther gave birth to Elizabeth Whitfield on April 17, while on the run.[18] The newborn was named after Dolphin's only sister.

A few days later, the Floyds were crossing the Brazos River when their cart overturned. Everything, including little Elizabeth, spilled into the water. Miraculously, Elizabeth wasn't hurt.[19]

Esther's return trip to Gonzales wasn't any easier, but fortune was on her side.

One day Esther and her family rambled up to the campsite of Thomas and Robert Hunter on the Neches River. She was accompanied by an old African-American woman and man. A young man named Uria Anderson was also in her party. He offered to drive her cart in exchange for her hauling his trunk.

Esther asked the Hunters for permission to camp with them, and the two brothers were pleased with the company.

A campfire provided the opportunity for everyone to tell of their adventures in the past months. Esther had a hard time talking. She told the Hunters her husband had been killed at the Alamo and she was trying to get back home. The Hunters offered their condolences. Then Esther began to cry. One of the wheels on her cart had rotted to pieces. She didn't know what to do.

Robert Hunter told her not to worry. He repaired the wheel by carving new spokes.

The Hunters joined Esther in the journey west, and this time she was pleased to have the company. The party encountered much difficulty in crossing the Neches River. At one point, the party came to a river crossing and the Hunters didn't have the $7 ferry fee to cross. Esther gladly loaned them the money.

The rickety cart was holding strong until they got into the East Texas pines, where the other wheel broke. An old man named Yoakum lived in the area, and he said he would sell Esther a wooden cart for $15. Esther declined the offer.

Robert Hunter again said he would repair the wheel, but Yoakum wouldn't allow any trees to be cut from his property. Robert and Anderson hiked back six miles to cut some timber for the job.

Eventually, the party was again trekking west.

Their long, grueling journey took them through the San Jacinto battlefield, where the harsh reality of the past year was clearly evident. The field was littered with the bones of Mexican soldiers.

The group eventually reached Robert Hunter's home near Fort Bend. After a short rest, Robert took Esther's cart and hewed off the surplus bark and wood to make it lighter.

Dr. Hunter, Thomas and Robert's father, took the time to prepare some food for the Floyds' remaining journey back to Gonzales. He ground five bushels of meal, killed a steer, and barbecued all the meat she wanted.

The cart carried Esther and her family back home safely. When she arrived, she wrote the Hunters a letter of thanks.[20]

Esther would later discover Dolphin died on March 6, 1836 — his thirty-second birthday.[21]

FRANCISCO VASQUEZ

Family Secret

Ramon Vasquez y Sanchez presented the oral evidence for the follow-ing story. Sanchez often heard this story from his grandmother, Maria Ybarra, about a great-great-grandfather who fought under Mexican Generalissimo Santa Anna at the Alamo.

From generation to generation, family members quietly passed down the story of Francisco Vasquez in bits and pieces until the details were fragmented and all but forgotten.

Vasquez was a Mexican *soldado* who fought under General-issimo Santa Anna at the time of the Texas Revolution. He was wounded March 6, 1836, as the Mexican Army victoriously crushed the Texas rebels at the Battle of the Alamo in San An-tonio de Bexar.

A local family housed the wounded Vasquez after the battle and cared for his wounds. In that time, Vasquez grew close to his new friends and eventually married into the family. He married Marcela Vasquez, and they lived in the *Paso de la Garza* area near the Medina River.

But Vasquez's exploits as a Mexican *soldado* were always kept hush-hush — even within family circles.

This is how Vasquez lived in peace in the shadow of the Alamo.[22]

SANTIAGO RABIA

Mexican Officer

Roger McMullen presented the oral evidence for the following story. McMullen is a great-grandson of Mexican officer Santiago Rabia (Ravia), who was a member of the Tampico Regiment.

Death came to Santiago Rabia without warning around 1853 in the Texas town of Nacogdoches. He died a loyal Texan and a veteran of the Texas Revolution.

Ironically, seventeen years earlier, Rabia marched on Texas soil under Mexican General Santa Anna in an effort to crush the territory's fight for independence. He was one of Santa Anna's loyal officers.[23]

Rabia's strange odyssey began in Spain, where as a youth he was strongly encouraged by his parents to become a Catholic priest. Ever since his birth in 1804 in the Spanish province of Bosque, Rabia was expected to someday join the priesthood.

Those plans changed drastically when Rabia was ten years old. Both of his parents died in 1814, and as a result, he migrated to Tampico, Mexico.

Rabia was placed in a military school in Mexico City when he came of age. Upon graduation, he became an officer under the esteemed Santa Anna.

War with the rebels in the Mexican province of Tejas eventually took Rabia north in the winter of 1836. He would witness the heroic stand of Texan forces at the Alamo and their mass slaughter by the onrushing Mexican *soldados*.

Rabia would also take part in the Battle of San Jacinto, where he was injured and eventually captured. Like a number of his comrades, Rabia was held captive at Galvez Island.

Texian officials, in time, gave Rabia an opportunity to earn his freedom. All he had to do was pledge his allegiance to the Republic of Texas, which he promptly did. When he took this oath he changed his name from Rabia to Ravia.

Santiago Ravia served four months in the Texas Army, and was awarded 640 acres in Nacogdoches for his services.[24]

The blond-haired, blue-eyed Spaniard fit in well with the flood of Anglo emigrants to Texas, and on July 8, 1841, he married an Irish girl named Carroll. The couple had seven children (Joseph, Alexander, Peter Celestine, Mary Margaret Lucinda, Mary Jane Lucinda, Mary Ann, and Pilar).

Roughly twelve years after his marriage to Carroll, Ravia's strange journey came to an even stranger end. He was killed in a family quarrel by one of his wife's brothers.[25]

GEORGE W. TUMLINSON

A Fightin' Tumlinson

Elizabeth Tumlinson Ashworth and Bobbie Rogers Thompson pre-
sented oral evidence for the following story. Both descend from John
Tumlinson, who was a brother of Alamo defender George W. Tum-
linson.

Texas was shaped by the toughest pioneer families, and
none was tougher than the Tumlinson clan.

Brothers James and John Tumlinson first arrived in Texas
from Arkansas as part of Moses Austin's Colony. From those two
brothers emerged a long line of fighting men who played major
roles in the history of Texas and the West.

John Tumlinson was credited by some with forming the
forerunners to the Texas Rangers. Joseph W. Tumlinson, the
first sheriff of Dimmit County, claimed to have killed twenty-one
outlaws. And then there was Frank Tumlinson, who according to
family legend, was once offered $500 to kill Wyatt Earp in
Dodge City. Frank would have finished the job, family members
boast, but Earp never showed up while the hired gun was in
town.

Still, no Tumlinson is more bragged about by kin than young
George Washington Tumlinson.

Tumlinsons take great pride in the fact that George was one
of the men who died March 6, 1836, at the Battle of the Alamo.
He was only twenty-two years old when he chose to make his
final stand for Texas independence.

George served the family name well.

At the Grass Fight and the Battle of Concepcion, George
and his brothers, James III and Littleton, were right in the middle of the scrap. George would eventually separate from his
brothers to take part in both the Siege and Battle of Bexar. He
later returned to the Alamo as part of the relief force from Gonzales.

James Tumlinson, Jr., George's father, was a freighter for

the Texas Army. At some point prior to March 6, James, Jr., left the Alamo with a note from his son to his stepbrother, John White. The family did not know at the time that the letter would be one of the last memories of George alive.

In true Tumlinson spirit, George went down fighting when the Mexican Army made its final assault on the Alamo.

George's death and the Alamo massacre stirred bad blood in his brothers. John, David C., and Littleton Tumlinson sought to avenge their brother's death at the Battle of San Jacinto.

Prior to the battle, Littleton was heard to say, "After we win this war, I will dance in the streets in a Mexican uniform and lady's hat." After the war, he did.

The Tumlinsons never forgot the Alamo, young George, or the men who fought by his side. They were well acquainted with a number of those Texas legends, especially the rough and tough James Bowie. Tumlinson men always laughed at the thought of Bowie. They often recalled how it was never wise to go drinking with Bowie because when he got drunk, he loved to pick fights and carve people up with his famed knife.

George's last stand was always a curiosity to the family. James Tumlinson, Jr., even traveled back to Bexar after the war to see if he could scrounge up any information about his son's death. He found Bowie's lover. She nursed Bowie until his death prior to the final assault, but didn't recall George Tumlinson. She suggested talking to Susanna Dickinson, who was in the Alamo chapel with her baby when the Mexican Army stormed the tiny mission fortress.

Dickinson told James about a young man who ran into the chapel during the final moments of the battle. His chin was shot and he desperately tried to give her a message for his family. Before the young man could relay his message, however, he ran out of the room and was never seen again.

James Tumlinson, Jr., believed that young man was George.

Years later, the family heard news of a skull found near the Alamo. The jawbone was mangled.

The Tumlinson clan figured they had finally found George.[26]

RAFAEL MORALES

Santa Anna's Scout

*Helena Benavides Townsend presented the oral evidence for the fol-
lowing story. Townsend is a great-granddaughter of Rafael Morales,
who served as a scout in Santa Anna's army in 1836. Townsend
heard stories about Morales from her grandmother, Maria de Jesus
Morales.*

Ashes from the cremated Alamo defenders swirled in the
wind around Bexar as scout Rafael Morales led the Mexican
Army east.

Morales was born and raised in Bexar, and went to his grave
claiming to have never participated in the Battle of the Alamo.
Yet he would never return home because of his role in the Texas
Revolution.

His strange odyssey was set in motion as a teenager in
Bexar. His mother, Carmen Balderas, remarried after the death
of Rafael's father, and she could never coax her son into liking
his stepfather. Their personalities always clashed.

Morales especially resented the fact that his stepfather insisted on being called "father," something Rafael could never
bring himself to do. His father was dead.

One day the tension between the two exploded for the last
time. Morales threw a chair at his stepfather, breaking it into
pieces. His mother was so furious, she chased Rafael out of the
house.

With nowhere to go, Morales remembered he had Comanche blood. As a child, whenever he was defiant or bad, his mother would always yell at him, "It must be the Comanche in you!"
Of course, she never mentioned that she was one-quarter Comanche herself.

Morales' great-grandfather, Ramon Balderas, was a captain
in the Spanish Army and had married a Comanche woman
while in Texas. At the time, relations were friendly between the
Spaniards and the Comanches. Morales was hopeful little had
changed.

So he went in search of his Comanche relatives. His journey led him to a great-uncle, who was his great-grandmother's brother and a respected chief among the feared tribe. The chief invited Morales to live in his lodge.

In time, Morales would learn the ways of the Comanche. Tracking, hunting, riding, and fighting were all part of his cultural training. But he would one day have to say goodbye to his new family as well. The chief wanted Morales to marry one of his great-granddaughters, and he refused. Morales had no other choice but to leave the tribe.

Revolution was looking like a certainty for Texas and Mexico about this time. Morales discovered his stepfather had joined the Texians, and out of pure dislike he quipped, "Well, I'm gonna have to join the Mexican Army because I'm not gonna be on his side."

Morales, at the age of twenty in 1836, kept his word.

Soon afterward the young Bexar native was working as a scout under Mexican General Santa Anna. He discovered his heart wasn't with either faction.

Actual battle would avoid Morales throughout most of his time in the war because of his status as a scout. Luck wasn't always a companion, though.

The haunting moment of one battle would never leave Morales. A group of Texians was captured after one conflict and ordered to be executed. Morales was one of the Mexicans chosen to serve on the firing squad. Reluctantly, Morales grabbed his rifle and moved into position, only to discover one of the Texians standing in front of him was a childhood friend from Bexar. A terrible feeling overcame Morales as his heart sank with grief.

Morales nonetheless fired upon command.

Other Texians who avoided execution watched the slaughter, and Morales believed they would tell of his role on the firing squad. He knew if he lived through the war, he could never return home and face his Bexar neighbors.

Events in the Texas Revolution seemed to come fast and furious for Morales, who one day found himself feeling uncomfortable with the location of the Mexican Army's camp. The Mexicans had set up tents near a river, and soldiers were leisurely walking around. Some, like Santa Anna himself, decided to take an afternoon nap.

Morales continued to feel uneasy. The strange feeling led him to Santa Anna's tent.

"Don't rest," Morales told Santa Anna. "Something is wrong. I know the Texians are coming. I know it. I feel it."

"Don't worry about it, Morales," Santa Anna replied. "Everything is under control. Let's take a nap today."

Sleep was the last thing on the mind of Morales. He began to snoop around camp, peeking into tents and scouting for any signs of danger. His instincts kept telling him to be on guard.

Finally, Morales entered a tent where the Mexicans kept barrels of gunpowder. He removed the lids of several barrels to check the contents. Under a few inches of gunpowder, Morales was shocked to find nothing more than sand.

Someone had sabotaged the gunpowder.

Morales immediately reported his findings to Santa Anna.

"Something is wrong," Morales told the Mexican general. "Someone is setting us up. There is no gunpowder. It is all sand."

"Don't worry about it, Morales," Santa Anna casually replied. "We're all right."

Gunshots suddenly cracked in the air as the Texas rebels caught the Mexicans by surprise. Morales and other Mexican soldiers scurried to meet the Texian assault. They were greeted by an overwhelming flurry of men who fought to avenge the deaths of their friends, neighbors, and fellow patriots. The Texians fought on adrenaline.

From the ranks, Morales and his fellow soldiers heard the Texians yell, "Remember the Alamo! Remember Goliad!"

The Mexicans resisted the best they could, but it proved a futile defense. With no gunpowder, they were reduced to fleeing for their lives. Some Mexican soldiers helplessly cried, "M' no Goliad! M' no Alamo!"

In roughly eighteen minutes, the battle was over. The Mexican province of Tejas was dead.

Morales was among the many Mexicans wounded in the furious battle, and he lay on the battlefield when a captain in the Texas Army walked by. The man was a cousin of Morales. He was shocked to see Morales had fought for Mexico.

"What are you doing here, cousin?" asked the Texas captain. "You don't belong here. You're a Texan."

Morales replied that he was unlucky enough to get mixed up with Santa Anna.

Fearing for Morales' safety, the captain helped carry his cousin over to the side of the Texian wounded. The captain placed his hat on Morales' head to conceal his identity.

Juan Seguin was the captain's name.

Morales never forgot how his famous cousin probably saved his life. Nor was he ever able to erase the awful memory of serving on the Mexican firing squad, a nightmare which haunted him until his death at age seventy.

After the war, Morales settled along the Mexican border in what is today the town of Brownsville. His final resting place is the Old Brownsville Cemetery, where he was buried fifty years after the end of the Texas Revolution.

Morales made a comfortable life for himself as a farmer and enjoyed raising a family. Still, he would always pay for his role in Santa Anna's army.

For the day Morales pulled the trigger was the day he knew he could never return home.[27]

WILLIAM DePRIEST SUTHERLAND

O, God Support Me

The letter in the following passage was written June 5, 1836, by Frances "Menefee" Sutherland to her sister, Sarah Norment, in Tennessee. Sutherland was the mother of Alamo defender William DePriest Sutherland.

Three months had passed before Frances "Menefee" Sutherland could work up the courage to write her sister, Sarah Norment, in Tennessee. Sutherland, wife of Maj. George Sutherland, was still reeling from the loss of her son, William DePriest Sutherland.

The seventeen-year-old William was among those who died at the Alamo.

With a pain in her heart and tears welling in her eyes, Mrs. Sutherland began to write:

June 5, 1836

Dear Sister,

I received your kind letter of some time in March, but never had it been my power to answer it 'til now, and now what I must say (O, God support me.) Yes, sister, I must say it to you, I have lost my William. O, yes he is gone, my poor boy is gone, gone from me. The sixth day of March in the morning, he was slain in the Alamo in San Antonio. Then his poor body committed to the flames. Oh, Sally, can you sympathize with and pray for me that I may have grace to help in this great time of trouble. He was there a volunteer, when the Mexican army came there. At the approach of thousands of enemies they had to retreat in the Alamo where they were quickly surrounded by the enemy. Poor fellows. The Mexicans kept nearly continual firing on them for thirteen days. Then scaled the walls and killed every man in the fort but two black men.

Dear Sister, I think the situation a sufficient excuse for not answering your letter sooner. Since I received your letter I had been away from home with a distracted mind and had got back to our house where we found nothing in the world worth speaking of — not one mouthful of anything to eat, but a little we brought home with us. God only knows how we will make out.

I will try to compose my mind while I give you a short history of a few months back: The American army was on our frontier. We thought prudent to stay at home and did so until the General (Sam Houston) thought proper to retreat. We, being on the frontier, were compelled to go (I speak for all.) We went to the Colorado, forty miles, but after some time, the General thought proper to retreat farther and of course we had to go, too. We proceeded to the Brazos River. There stopped a few days, but dread and fear caused another start; there Mr. Sutherland quit us and joined the army. William Heard was in, also, with a good many more of our citizens, however, we went on for several miles and again stopped, hoping we would not have to go farther, but someone over there that week brought in the early news the Mexican army was crossing the Brazos not more than forty miles behind us. Again we started and traveled two days then heard the army was twenty miles behind. (I wish you could know how the people did as they kept going about trying to get somewhere, but no person knew where they were going to get to.) Several weeks passed on without any certain account from the army. All this time you could hardly guess my feelings. My poor William gone, Sutherland in the army, me with my three little daughters and my poor Thomas wandering about, not knowing what to do or where to go. You will guess my feelings were dreadful, but ever the Lord supported me, and was on our side for I think I may boldly say the Lord fought our battles. Only to think how many thousands of musket and cannon balls were flying there over our army and so few touched. I think seven was all that died of their wounds. Some say our army fought double their number and who dares say that the Lord was not on our side. Mr. Sutherland's horse was killed under him, but the Lord preserved his life and brought him back to his family. He found us at the mouth of the Sabine from thence we all returned home. I pray that God will still continue our friend and bless us with peace again. . . .[28]

WILLIAM IRVINE LEWIS

Final Request

The letter in the following passage was written by Texan General Sam Houston July 24, 1836, to Mary B. Lewis in Pennsylvania. Lewis was the mother of Alamo defender William Irvine Lewis.

San Augustine, Texas, 24th, July, 1836

[To Mrs. Mary B. Lewis of Philadelphia]

Madam,

Yours of the 7th —: has been received in answer to which I am sorry to inform you that I am unable at this time to give you any definite information in regard to your son William I. Lewis. I have examined the rolls of the army of San Jacinto in which his name does not appear — I am fearful he joined within the Command of Colonels Fannin of Travis, and had shared the fate of the brave men who fell at La Bahia & the Alamo: of this — I am not certain, for I have never been furnished with the Muster Rolls of those Commands, and as some of Fannin's men escaped, it is possible he may be among them — I will make further inquires and should I obtain any facts relating to his fate, I shall take pleasure in communicating them to you. Be assured madam that I — sympathize with you in your sorrow and anxiety for the supposed bereavement of a brave son, who nobly volunteered in the Cause of Freedom, in — of a people struggling against tyranny and oppresion.

I have the honor to bid
with great respect

Yours Truly,
Sam Houston[29]

The worst fears of Mary B. Lewis were later realized. Through her constant inquires, she learned of her son's death at the Alamo on March 6, 1836. She also discovered through the grapevine that a few possessions belonging to the Alamo slain had been recovered. Thus, she made one final request to the people of Texas.

Mary wrote to the Texas government and asked if any item of William's had been found, and if it could be sent home as a memento. Her heartfelt request was reported in *The Telegraph and Texas Register* on October 21, 1840:

His mother hearing that a few articles belonging to that gallant, though ill fated band of patriots had been recovered, wrote to a gentleman of this city, to procure if possible, something which had belonged to her son, that she might keep it in perpetual rememberence of him.

The information upon which her request was predicated was incorrect. Nothing has been preserved of those gallant spirits. . . .[30]

The people of Texas hardly ignored Mary's request. A piece of the Alamo ruins was retrieved and sculpted especially for her. On the rock was engraved the name of her Alamo hero: "Lewis."[31]

MIAL SCURLOCK

Old Comrades

The following story is based on Essie Walton Martin's "The Scur-locks: Seekers of Freedom." Martin is a great-granddaughter of Capt. William Scurlock, a brother of Alamo defender Mial Scurlock.

William Scurlock rode his horse up to the front gate of the Jacksonville, Texas, ranch, and peered down at the little boy playing in the front yard. The year was 1873.

"Does Ned Ragsdale live here?"

"Yes," the boy said to the stranger.

"Is that him on the gallery?" continued Scurlock, pointing to the man on the front porch.

The boy nodded.

"Tell him to come here."

Scurlock smiled as he began to dismount. Ned Ragsdale rose from his chair on the porch and slowly walked toward the stranger. Ragsdale told the man he was welcome to stay the night as he moved closer, but was then interrupted.

"Ned," Scurlock said, "do you know me?"

"Take off your hat," Ragsdale said with a curious expression.

Scurlock obliged, exposing his bald head.

"Bill Scurlock!" hollered Ragsdale as he threw his arms around his old friend.

Thirty-seven years had elapsed since the two were together in the Texas War for Independence. They had been separated at the Goliad Massacre of 1836, and each thought the other had died in the slaughter.

Now they were embracing on a warm Saturday afternoon in

Texas, and a full minute passed before the two men broke their bond.

Silence fell on the two old comrades as they made their way to the house some thirty paces away. They were choked with emotion.

Once inside the house, memories of the old days came rushing back. So did the thought of all those years of grieving. They couldn't help but shake their heads in disbelief.

Wasn't it just yesterday they used to take their "fire pans" — flintlock rifles — on all-night deer hunts? Where did the years go? Why couldn't things have worked out differently? But the conversation always led back to, "It's so good to see you, old friend."

They even laughed when they recalled the hunt in which Scurlock severely burned his scalp trying to rekindle a "fire pan." That was why Ragsdale had asked him to take off his hat at the gate. Only William Scurlock would have a scarred, bald scalp.

One story followed another well into the night. Nimrod Ragsdale, the boy who greeted Scurlock, listened intently to every word. Eventually, the stories led to the Texas War for Independence.

They relived the adventure, the excitement, the good times, and most of all, the sorrow for those comrades who fell in battle. Scurlock had vowed never to forget. After all, he had lost a brother at the Alamo.

So with a heavy heart, he remembered . . .

*   *   *

In 1834, word reached William and his brother, Mial, in Tennessee about the vast amounts of land given to settlers in Mexico. So impressed were the Scurlock brothers, they decided to leave immediately for the Mexican province of Tejas.

They departed for Texas with a slave man, a slave woman, her four-year-old boy, and supplies. Along the way, they saw abandoned houses with "G.T.T." (Gone To Texas) scrawled on the doors.

The Scurlocks made their way through Louisiana, crossed the Sabine River on Gaines Ferry, and eventually settled in the town of San Augustine. It was there Dr. Samuel Thompson, *alcalde,* helped William get his land grant of 640 acres in the Sabine District.

William, the slave woman, and her son lived in a San Augustine hotel initially. The woman worked in the hotel, while William paid their bill by supplying wild game for the dinner table.

Mial and the slave man, meanwhile, cleared the newly acquired land and built a log cabin. Late in 1834, the five immigrants moved onto the land.[32]

When disputes between Mexico and the Texas settlers heated, Mial and William were among the first to volunteer for duty in the Texas Army. They officially committed their services October 17, 1835, in San Augustine, leaving their slaves in the care of a friend.

The Scurlock brothers would fight side by side at the Battle of Concepcion, the Grass Fight, and the Battle of Bexar before being separated.

At the Battle of Concepcion, William took his flintlock rifle and scouted along the San Antonio River. He heard a jingling noise and quickly ducked into the cover of the brush. A Mexican officer appeared, mounted on a horse. He, too, was on a scouting mission.

The jingling noise was caused by the Mexican's big spurs and sword, which did him no good when he peered behind the tree covering William. The experienced Tennessee hunter shot the Mexican dead, prompting his horse to gallop off in the direction of Bexar without a rider.

William and Mial again went into battle November 26 in the Grass Fight and two weeks later at the Battle and Siege of Bexar. On December 10, after a bloody hand-to-hand, house-to-house fight, Mexican Brigadier General Martin Perfecto de Cos surrendered the tiny mission fortress called the Alamo. The two brothers rejoiced in the glory of victory.

But the celebration was short.

Dr. James Grant and F.W. Johnson were leading a force to take Matamoros by mid-January. William Scurlock was one of the roughly 200 men enlisted for the expedition. Mial remained at the Alamo as a rifleman.

The Matamoros Expedition proved to be a disaster. Mexican forces surrounded the Texians at Agua Dulce Creek on March 2 and soundly defeated them. As fate would have it, William and a Mexican man were rounding up horses at the time of the battle and were among the few who escaped.

Mial and the other Alamo defenders, meanwhile, had already held off the main Mexican force for nine days.

William eventually made his way through the dangerous countryside back to Goliad, where he joined Col. James Fannin's regiment. There he first heard the devastating news of the Alamo massacre and the death of his brother. Buddies Ned and Peter Ragsdale delivered the sad news.

Revenge filled William's heart, and his attention quickly turned back to the battlefield.

William's next moment of truth came during Fannin's retreat. Fannin and roughly 300 of his men slipped out of Goliad en route for Victoria. The news was that 1,500 Mexican troops were bearing down on Goliad and the Texians had to move quickly.

Peter Ragsdale was sent to round up beef for the men, while his brother, Ned, was stricken with the chills and assigned to escort the women and children to safety. William hastily said goodbye to his friends before marching out.

The entire company was in a rush.

In all the confusion of the flight, no food was taken. This would prove costly when Fannin ordered a halt to the march in the wide-open prairie at Coleto Creek. Officers insisted on reaching the cover of the nearby timberline, where water could also be obtained from the creek. But Fannin stood by his decision. Scurlock, now a captain, was among those in the middle of the debate.

The argument became moot when Mexican soldiers emerged from the bushes and trees and surrounded Fannin's army. A heavy spray of gunfire was soon being exchanged.

Scurlock and the other men circled the wagons and carts. They piled the dead livestock for protection, and the fighting, which started in the afternoon, lasted well into the night.

Reinforcements arrived before long and the Mexican forces were said to be 1,000 strong. Food and water, however, would be the greatest disadvantage for the Texians.

The next morning, on March 20, Colonel Fannin and his

men surrendered. They were told they would be sent to New Orleans on parole.

Seven days later, on Palm Sunday, Santa Anna ordered their execution.[33]

Captain Scurlock was among the few spared.

Scurlock had spent several years studying medicine back East, and was selected by a Mexican doctor to care for the sick and wounded. When the doctor realized the Texians were being sent to their death, he took Scurlock to his tent and had him crawl under his cot. Blankets were then dropped down on both sides of the cot to conceal Scurlock, and the doctor told him not to move.

Scurlock had no idea what was about to happen. He then heard gunfire.

Frightened, Scurlock slid out from under the cot and lifted the canvas at the bottom of the tent. He saw a white man running toward the camp with two Mexican cavalrymen in pursuit. One of the Mexicans overtook the man and swiped at him with his lancer. The man narrowly missed being clipped when he darted underneath the horse, causing the lancer to tangle with the horse's legs. The horse reared back, bucked the Mexican from his saddle, and galloped away toward the camp. The horse began to slow as it reached a row of tents.

Scurlock, realizing what was taking place, seized the opportunity to escape. He scrambled from the tent to grab the horse's bridle, mounted, and dashed off. He rode until the horse gave out, and then ditched the saddle and bridle before setting the horse loose.

Traveling by night and resting during the day, Scurlock eventually crossed paths with another Texian refugee. They were both trying to reach General Houston's army. The two Texians traveled by the stars, but eventually parted when they disagreed on what direction to take to meet Houston.[34]

Scurlock was again captured en route to San Augustine. This time two Mexicans hunted him down, and one threatened to kill him. The other prevailed in sparing the captain's life, and instead insisted on returning him to the Mexican Army. He took the captain to his home, where he was locked in a small, dark room.

The exhausted Scurlock was fed by the wife of his Mexican captor, and he succeeded in winning her sympathy with tales of his hardships. Before long, after a lengthy discussion, the couple set Scurlock free.

Mial's death was again on his mind. Determined to avenge the loss of his brother, the captain marched to San Augustine, where a petition had been filed against his estate due to a report about his supposed death. But there was no time for legal papers.

The captain rounded up a company of volunteers and dashed off to meet Houston at San Jacinto.

Alas, Scurlock arrived too late for the battle. Santa Anna's army was already defeated. Scurlock still proudly took part in the clean-up work. His thoughts then turned to the future.

Depression set in when Scurlock returned to his home in the Sabine District later that year. Everywhere he turned, he found himself alone. Mial was gone forever, the Ragsdale brothers were nowhere to be found, and neither was his sweetheart, Frances Thompson. Frances and her family had evidently packed up and left the country.

Sad, lonely and depressed, Scurlock was determined to start anew. He, too, decided to leave. Mounting his horse, he headed east toward Louisiana.

As nightfall closed in on that first day of travel, Scurlock stopped at a house to inquire about quarters for the night. A woman came to the door — his sweetheart's mother — but he held his tongue. The lady, who didn't recognize William, invited him to supper. He gladly obliged.

When Frances entered the dining room that night, William stood.

"Frances," he said, "don't you recognize me?"

William and Frances were married one month later, on November 9, 1836.

*   *   *

Ned Ragsdale shook his head in disbelief. He still couldn't believe his old comrade was alive. Incredible, he thought. Simply incredible.

The two were emotionally drained from the stories, but hardly tired. They had thirty-seven years to catch up on. Still,

there was nothing like recalling the good ol' days, and the conversation quickly shifted to their all-night hunts.

Once, one of them crippled a deer with a shot. When the
deer darted into the woods, they threw down their rifles and
joined in the chase. They returned to discover that a "fire pan"
had sparked a fire and burned to the stock on one of the rifles.
Ned later replaced the stock on the rifle, and thirty-seven years
later, that same rifle stood in the corner of his front room.

William spotted the rifle and squeezed it with his hands.
Captain Scurlock began to cry.[35]

NOTES

Preface

1. Alex Haley, *Roots* (New York: Doubleday, 1976), 578–579.

Part I: Date with Destiny

1. Stephen L. Hardin, *Texian Iliad: A Military History of the Texas Revolution* (Austin: University of Texas Press, 1994), 155.

2. Jose Enrique de la Pena, *With Santa Anna in Texas: A Personal Narrative of the Revolution* (College Station: Texas A&M University Press, 1975), 54-55.

3. Robert M. Utley, *The Lance and the Shield: The Life and Times of Sitting Bull* (New York: Henry Holt and Company, 1993), 149.

4. Harry Albright, *New Orleans: The Battle of the Bayous* (New York: Hippocrene Books, 1990), 161.

5. Daniel W. Cloud, letter to his brother, John B. Cloud, 26 December 1835. The original letter is in a vault at the Daughters of the Republic of Texas Library at the Alamo, San Antonio, Texas. It was presented to the DRT by descendants of Cloud at a meeting of the Cloud Family Association held in DeGray State Park in Arkadelphia, Arkansas, in 1979. All descendants of his heirs present at the meeting signed a document of transmittal.

6. Ralph W. Steen, "Letter from San Antonio de Bexar in 1836," *Southwestern Historical Quarterly* 62:513-518; and William R. Carey to brother and sister, 12 January 1836, John H. Jenkins, ed., *Papers of the Texas Revolution* (Austin: Presidial Press, 1973), 3:494.

7. Mark Deer, *The Frontiersman: The Real Life and the Many Legends of Davy Crockett* (New York: William Morrow and Company, Inc., 1993), 222; Davy Crockett's 1835 Almanack of Wild Sports of the West, and *Life in the Backwoods* (Nashville: Snag & Sawyer), 2.

8. James Wakefield Burke, *David Crockett: The Man Behind the Myth* (Austin: Eakin Press, 1984), 197.

9. Gary S. Zaboly, "Crockett Goes to Texas: A Newspaper Chronology," *Alamo Battlefield Association Journal*, No. 1 (Summer 1995): 10.

10. John Sutherland, *The Fall of the Alamo* (San Antonio: The Naylor Company, 1935), 11-12.

11. John Sowers Brooks, letter to his father, 2 March 1836. Printed in Jenkins, *Letters,* 4:487.

12. Andrew Jackson Kent's age, along with those of his wife and ten children, listed in the Bible of William Riley Billings, a great-grandson of the Alamo hero. Kent's birthday is listed as December 25, 1791. Mary Ann Kent was born December 16, 1827.

13. David Kent was born February 23, 1817, according to the family Bible of William Riley Billings.

14. David Kent told this to his niece, Henrietta Clark. The story was collected and documented by Chester P. Wilkes for the Kent family reunions. Wilkes' wife, Doris, is the great-great-great-granddaughter of Andrew Kent.

15. Mary Ann Kent told the story of Ben Highsmith escaping danger at Powder House Hill to her grandson, Oliver Byas. The story was passed on to Chester P. Wilkes.

16. Mary Ann Kent told this story of being awakened by cannon blasts on the morning of March 6, 1836 to many. The story was passed on to Chester P. Wilkes.

17. Birdie Clark said David Kent told this to Sarah E. Dillard. Clark is a great-great-great-granddaughter of Andrew Kent. Dillard is his great-niece. Stories of Gen. Sam Houston's arrival to Gonzales, David Kent's orders to ride for Goliad with a letter, Anselmo Borgara's and Andres Barcena's arrest and "Deaf" Smith's return were passed on to Chester P. Wilkes.

18. Oral evidence for this story was presented by Chester P. Wilkes. He has spent years preserving the legends of the Kent family.

19. Susan Alice Cargile, telephone interview with author, Dallas, Texas, 19 June 1995. Cargile is a great-great-granddaughter of John Henry Dillard, and she grew up with many of Granny Hickey's family legends.

20. G. A. McCall, "William T. Malone," *Quarterly of the Texas State Historical Association* 14, no. 4 (April 1911): 325-326.

21. *Malone et al v. Moran et al.,* number 3644, on file in the district court of Parker County, Texas. Copy in the miscellaneous file of William T. Malone at the DRT Library.

22. Frances Araiza, telephone interview with author, San Antonio, Texas, 19 July 1995. Araiza was told stories about Ruiz by her grandmother, Demetria Ruiz, when she was a little girl. Her grandmother often referred to the *soldado* as her "father," but Araiza suspects she meant "grandfather." So Araiza is either a great-granddaughter or great-great-granddaughter to the *soldado* in Gen. Antonio Lopez de Santa Anna's army. Araiza could not remember the *soldado*'s first name.

23. Mary Autry Greer, "Major M. Autry: Sketch of Father's life." Copy in Micajah Autry's file at the DRT Library.

24. Micajah Autry to Martha Autry, 7 December 1835. *Quarterly of the Texas State Historical Association* 14, no. 4 (April 1911): 317-318.

25. Micajah Autry to Martha Autry, 13 December 1835. *Quarterly of the Texas State Historical Association* 14, no. 4 (April 1911): 318-319.

26. Micajah Autry to Martha Autry, 13 January 1836. *Quarterly of the Texas State Historical Association* 14, no. 4 (April 1911): 319-320.

27. Greer, "Major M. Autry: Sketch of Father's life."

28. Death announcement reprinted in the *Jackson Mississippian*, 6 May 1836, from the *Russellville Advertiser.* Copy in Daniel W. Cloud's file at the DRT Library.

29. Daniel W. Cloud to John B. Cloud, 26 December 1835.

30. Pat Cloud, telephone interview with author, Austin, Texas, 17 August 1994. Cloud and her husband, Robert, originally heard the story in 1978 from Clarissa Cloud's grandson, Edward Coffman, of Russellville, Kentucky. Robert Cloud is Daniel W. Cloud's great-great-great-nephew.

31. Minnie Shelton, telephone interview with author, Gonzales, Texas, 27 July 1995. Shelton is a great-niece of William P. King. She heard the story of his heroic decision as a child from her grandmother, Minnie Foster.

32. King Family Bible, typescript in King file at the DRT Library.

33. Steen, "Letter from San Antonio de Bexar in 1836," *Southwestern Historical Quarterly* 62:513-518; and Carey to brother and sister, 12 January 1836, Jenkins, *Papers,* 3:494.

The letter was addressed to Carey's brother-in-law, William F. Oppelt, and was mailed at Natchitoches on 7 February 1836.

34. David P. Cummings to his father, 20 January 1836. Printed in Jenkins, *Papers,* 4:86-87.

35. David P. Cummings to his father, 14 February 1836. Printed in Jenkins, *Papers,* 4:333-334.

36. Virginia Bronson, telephone interview with author, Fort Smith, Arkansas, 2 June 1995. Bronson is a great-great-great-great-granddaughter of Siden H. Harris, who according to family legend was an uncle to John Harris.

Documentation has never been found to verify the family legend. "The story has been handed down in our family for over 100 years," Bronson said. "So I would think there's something to the story."

37. Ralph Love, telephone interview with author, Georgetown, Texas, 20 August 1994. Love is a great-great-great-nephew of George Washington Cottle and a great-great-grandson of Zebulon Pike Cottle.

38. Billie Matthews, letter to author, 20 August 1994. Matthews is a great-great-great niece of George Washington Cottle and a great-great-granddaughter of Zebulon Pike Cottle.

39. Mabel Hitt to Ms. Hansell, 16 September 1975. The story of William Wells, Sr., becoming "despondent over his wife's death" comes from Hitt's letter. Hitt's husband, Rabon, is a great-great-grandson of William Wells, Sr. A copy of the letter is in the Wells' file at the DRT Library.

40. Dodie Pugh and William Austin Pugh, Jr., telephone interview with author, Mineola, Texas, 17 April 1995. Both told the story of the attorney tracking down William Wells, Jr. William Austin Pugh, Jr., is a great-great-great-grandson of William Wells, Sr.

41. Pughs, interview. David Crockett's discovery of a sleeping William Wells, Sr., in the hollow of a tree was told to the Pughs by an uncle, John

"Tink" Annison Wells. "Uncle Tink," who knew William Wells, Jr., died 28 February 1983 at the age of 100.

42. Pughs, interview. The story of Crockett joining the campsite of William Wells, Sr., was also told by Mabel Hitt in a letter of 16 September 1975 to writer Mrs. Hansell of San Antonio.

43. Matilda Crockett Fields, interview, no date, in the David Crockett miscellaneous file, DRT Library.

44. Isaac N. Jones to Elizabeth Crockett, 12 August 1836, reprinted in *Randolph Recorder*.

45. Burke, *David Crockett: The Man Behind The Myth*, 115-117.

46. David Crockett to daughter, 9 January 1836, printed in Jenkins, *Papers*, 3:453.

47. Mrs. H. Clay Johnson, *The Dallas Morning News*, 26 July 1925.

48. Frances Kerr John, telephone interview with author, Sugar Land, Texas, 14 July 1994. John is the great-great-great-granddaughter of David and Elizabeth Crockett.

49. Tylene Edminston, telephone interview with author, Georgetown, Texas, 16 April 1995. Edminston has gathered various legends from numerous family members of the McGregor clan. According to family legend, John McGregor had a brother. This has never been documented. Yet this is the story which has survived for generations. If true, John McGregor would be a distant uncle to Edminston.

50. R. L. Sowell, letter to Mr. Long, 23 June 1981. Copy in Andrew Jackson Sowell's file at the DRT Library. R. L. Sowell is a great-great-great-grandnephew of Andrew Jackson Sowell.

51. Lyle Saxon, *Lafitte the Pirate* (Gretna, La., 1989), 215-216.

52. Regina Pierce, telephone interview with author, tape recording, Dallas, Texas, 7 July 1994. Pierce, born in 1898, talked about the family legend concerning her great-great-uncle, Anthony Wolf. She first heard stories about Wolf from her uncle, Dave Wolf, who lived in Galveston, Texas.

53. Saxon, *Lafitte the Pirate*, 216-217.

54. *Ibid.*, 257.

55. Charles W. Evers to unidentified Ohio newspaper, 14 March 1878, printed in *San Antonio Express*, 24 February 1929.

Part II: Inside the Walls

1. William Fairfax Gray, *From Virginia to Texas, 1835: Diary of Col. Wm. F. Gray* (Houston: The Fletcher Young Publishing Co., 1965), 128-129.

2. *Ibid.*, 130.

3. Hardin, *Texas Illiad*, 163.

4. Gray, *From Virginia to Texas*, 136-137.

5. Unidentified Mexican *soldado* to "Brothers of my heart," 7 March 1836. *El Mosquito Mexicano*, 5 April 1836. Copy in DRT Library.

6. Lon Tinkle, *13 Days to Glory* (College Station: Texas A&M University Press, 1985), 244.

7. De la Pena, *With Santa Anna in Texas*, 52.

8. "Document Reveals Possible Survivor of Alamo Massacre," *Victoria Advocate,* 18 July 1985.

9. William B. Travis to the People of Texas, 23 February 1836, Archives Division, Texas State Library, Austin, reprinted in Jenkins, *Papers,* 4:423.

10. William B. Travis to [David Ayers], 3 March 1836, Texas Monument, 31 March 1852, printed in Jenkins, *Papers,* 4:501.

11. Adolph Herrera, interview with author, tape recording, San Antonio, Texas, 10 June 1994. Herrera is a great-great-grandson of Blas Herrera.

12. Albert Seguin-Carvajal Gonzales, letter to author, 6 July 1995. Gonzales opened his letter with, "My maternal grandmother, Maria Lucrecia Seguin-Carvajal Ramirez . . . was handed down the following story by word of mouth." Gonzales is a great-great-great-grandson of Juan Seguin.

13. Ellen Maverick Dickson, telephone interview with author, San Antonio, Texas, 16 April 1995. Dickson remembered hearing stories of Mary A. Maverick's height (well over six feet). Dickson is a great-granddaughter of Mary and Samuel Maverick.

14. Rena M. Green, *Memoirs of Mary A. Maverick: San Antonio's First American Woman* (San Antonio: Alamo Printing Co. 1921), 109.

15. *Ibid.,* 133-134.

16. Ellen Maverick Dickson, letter to author, 12 April 1995.

17. Donald Ottinger, telephone interview with author, Odessa, Texas, 7 April 1995. Ottinger, a great-grandson of James Wilson Nichols, said his mother, Lula McDoniel, grew up with the same story of Nichols being a butcher at the Alamo.

18. James Wilson Nichols, *Now You Hear My Horn: The Journal of James Wilson Nichols 1820-1887,* edited by Catherine W. McDowell (Austin: University of Texas Press, 1967).

19. *Ibid.,* 13-14.

20. Robert H. Davis, date unknown, unidentified Houston newspaper. Davis reported the legend of Allen's ride in an interview with F. C. Proctor, who as a fourteen-year-old heard the story from Allen, then a judge. Proctor claims the story was later verified by Allen's daughter, Mary L. Cunningham, of Yoakum, Texas.

21. William P. Zuber, *Sketch of Tapley Holland: A Heroe of the Alamo, March 6, 1836* (unpublished, 1910). Zuber's work was addressed to Amelia Martin of Anderson, Texas. He opens his sketch by writing, "Many of the facts herein stated were known to me at or near the times of their occurrence. For the rest, I am mainly indebted to Mr. Holland's sister, Mrs. Nancy Berryman, who stated them to me in conversation."

22. Pat Baimbridge, telephone interview with author, tape recording, McQueeney, Texas, 15 April 1995. Baimbridge grew up hearing stories of Louis "Moses" Rose from his grandmother, Ethylene Janelle Rose Baimbridge. Pat Baimbridge is a great-great-great-nephew of Rose.

Ethylene Janelle Rose Baimbridge once donated a pistol that belonged to Rose to the Alamo museum.

23. James Butler Bonham to Sam Houston, 1 December 1835.

24. Milledge Louis Bonham, "The Life and Times of Milledge Luke Bonham," 93-108. Copy at the University of South Carolina.

25. "Why Bonham Chose To Die With Travis," *Dallas Morning News,* 8 March 1931. While laced with an abundance of romance and heroism, the basis of Jan Isbelle Fortune's article was nonetheless taken from family accounts passed down to Mrs. Edger Wade, a great-great-great niece of James Butler Bonham. Unfortunately, Mrs. Wade compiled her family legends about Bonham in a play called "Dawn," which undoubtedly left history at the mercy of overdramatization.

26. Bonham, "The Life and Times of Milledge Luke Bonham," 93-108.

27. Dorothy Perez, telephone interview with author, Universal, Texas, 26 March 1995. Perez, Alejo Perez, Jr.'s great-granddaughter, first heard the story when she was about twelve years old from her aunt, Mamie Sosa. In the original story, Alejo was said to be twelve years old at the time. This, of course, was incorrect. Alejo was born 23 March 1835, and was seventeen days shy of his first birthday when the Alamo fell.

George Newton Perez, Dorothy's father, lived with Alejo for a short time before his death on 21 October 1918. Perez was just nine when his grandfather came to live with his family.

"My father and grandfather never said anything about the Alamo battle," George Perez recalled in a 1995 interview. "All they ever mentioned was that we descended from the Canary Islanders. That's all they ever passed on to me. My grandfather didn't think the Alamo battle would become so big in history."

28. Jessie McIlroy Smith, "Sarah Vauchere Walker's 70 Years on the Texas Frontier," date unknown, copy in Jacob Walker file, DRT Library. Smith is a great-granddaughter of Sarah Ann.

29. Bill Groneman, *Alamo Defenders, A Genealogy: The People and Their Words* (Austin: Eakin Press, 1990), 117.

30. Jessie McIlroy Smith, telephone interview with author, Austin, Texas, 8 April 1995. The story of Sarah Ann Vauchere Walker's ride, which has sometimes been called a 200-mile journey, was told to Smith along with other family legends by her grandmother, Rebecca Walker Adams. Rebecca was a daughter of Sarah Ann and her second husband, who was known as Jacob Walker II. He was a relative of the Alamo hero.

31. Smith, interview. Like her grandmother, Rebecca Walker Adams, Smith said the story of Jacob Walker's final moments is her favorite family story.

The family may have been told this story directly from Susanna Dickinson, who survived the battle. The family may have picked up the story, however, from M. J. Morphis' 1875 publication, *History of Texas.* On page 176 of that book, Morphis quotes Dickinson as saying, "I will now describe the memorable fall of the Alamo on Feb. 23, 1836 . . . Soon after he [Capt. Almeron Dickinson] left me, three unarmed gunners who abandoned their then useless guns came into the church where I was and were shot down by my side. One of them was from Nacogdoches and named Walker. He spoke to me several times during the siege about his wife and four children with anxious tenderness. I saw four Mexicans toss him up in the air, as you would a bundle of fodder with their bayonets, and then shoot him."

32. Court of Claims Voucher, no. 400, File (S-Z), General Land Office of Texas, Austin, cited in Amelia M. Williams, "A Critical Study," 4:283.

33. *Ibid.*

34. "Document Reveals Possible Survivor of Alamo Massacre," *Victoria Advocate,* 18 July 1985. The article states, "While sifting through information at the Texas State Land Office in Austin, [historian Kevin] Young found an affidavit written in behalf of the Warnell Family.

"The legal document, filed in July 1858, revealed that Warnell died less than three months after the fall of the Alamo from wounds he had received in combat.

"The document said Warnell died in Port Lavaca. But, pointing to the fact that the document was filed years after Warnell's death, Young believes that could be a loose reference to Dimmit's Landing."

35. Kevin L. Wornell has gathered many family legends in his travels. The basis for this story on Henry Warnell comes from Wornell's interview in the late 1970s with a distant cousin, Eydith Wornell Roach, of Arkansas. Roach was ninety-three at the time of the interview. Wornell believes he is a distant relative of the Alamo defender, but has never been able to prove it with documentation.

36. Howard R. Driggs, *Rise of the Lone Star: A Story told by Its Pioneers* (New York: Frederck A. Stokes Company), 213.

37. *Ibid.,* 225.

38. Enrique Esparza, "Alamo's Only Survivor," *San Antonio Express,* 12 May 1907.

39. *Ibid.,* 19 May 1907.

40. George R. Benavides, interview with author, San Antonio, Texas, 5 March 1995. Benavides was told the story by his grandmother, Margarita Sotelo Rosales, in 1967. Rosales didn't remember names when she told the story, but Benavides was able to match the names with the story years later through research.

"I was in fifth-grade at the time and my grandmother asked me in Spanish what I was studying," Benavides recalled. "I said, 'The Alamo.' She said I had an ancestor who died at the Alamo. I automatically thought he fought on the Mexican side. Our textbooks just said it was the Texans versus the Mexicans. We were never told Mexicans fought on the side of Texas.

"But my grandmother said, 'No, he fought on the Texas side and don't you forget it.' I just kind of brushed the story aside. I thought, 'How could a textbook be wrong?' But the story was true. My grandmother was right."

41. Richard D. Esparza. "Brothers at Arms," San Antonio, Texas, 1992. Esparza is the great-great-great-grandson of Francisco Esparza. He heard stories about his famous ancestor from his grandfather, Juan Antonio Esparza, Jr.

42. Martha Jane (Highsmith) O'Brien and Mary Deborah (Highsmith) O'Brien wrote a memorial to their father, Benjamin Franklin Highsmith. Typescript of memorial in Highsmith's miscellaneous file at the DRT Library at the Alamo, San Antonio, Texas.

43. Trinidad Coy, "New Light on Alamo Massacre," *San Antonio Light,* 26 November 1911.

44. Evelyn M. Carrington, ed., *Women in Early Texas* (Austin: American Association of University Women Austin Branch, 1975), 75. In the book, a short story is written on Susanna Wilkerson Dickinson by Willard Griffith Nitschke. Dickinson was Nitschke's great-grandmother.

45. Charles Ramsdell, *San Antonio: A Historical and Pictorial Guide* (Austin: University of Texas Press, 1959), 68.

46. Paul Griffith, telephone interview with author, Austin, Texas, 16 August 1994. Griffth is a great-great-grandson of Susanna and Almeron Dickinson.

47. Susanna Dickinson Hannig, "Alamo Remembered: 'Messenger of Death' made home in Lockhart following battle," by B. J. Benefiel, Mayor Pro-Tem, City of Luling, 6 March 1986.

48. Carrington, *Women in Early Texas,* 74.

49. Almarion Dickinson Griffith, "Hero's Kin, 83, Hears Alamo Ceremony," by Richard M. Morehead, United Press Staff Correspondent, date unknown.

50. *Ibid.*

51. Carrington, *Women in Early Texas,* 75.

Part III: Out of the Ashes
1. Walter Lord, *A Time To Stand* (New York: Harper & Brothers, 1961), 167.

2. Francis Antonio Ruiz, "The Fall of the Alamo, And Massacre of Travis and His Brave Associates," *Plum Creek Almanac,* Vol. 12, No. 1 (Spring 1994): 20-21. Translated by J. A. Quintero. The account was taken from the Texas Almanac of 1860. Copy in the files of the DRT Library.

3. Linda Halliburton, telephone interview with author, tape recording, Luling, Texas, 26 June 1994. Halliburton used to hear Alamo stories as a child from her great-grandmother, Rhoda Elizabeth Kimble Hurt, a granddaughter of George C. Kimble. Halliburton is Kimble's great-great-great-granddaughter.

4. Cordella Truesdell, telephone interview with author, Uvalde, Texas, 12 July 1994. Truesdell is a great-great-granddaughter of John W. Smith.

5. John Holland Jenkins III, ed., *Recollections of Early Texas: Memoirs of John Holland Jenkins* (Austin: University of Texas Press, 1958), 44.

6. Lee Spencer, paper presented to the Alamo Heroes Chapter on the grounds of the shrine at Alamo Hall, 4 January 1994. Spencer is the great-great-great-great-great-granddaughter of Gordon C. Jennings.

7. Janelle Sewell, telephone interview with author, tape recording, Dale, Texas, 3 August 1994. Sewell is a great-great-great-granddaughter of James George.

8. Pat Cloud, telephone interview with author, Austin, Texas, 17 August 1994. Cloud is the great-great-great-granddaughter of Sampson Connell. She was also told about the daring flight of Sarah Jane Clark's family by an aunt, Christine Elliott, who lived from 1905 to 1986. "When I asked my aunt [Elliott]

for any family information, she told me she didn't know anything except she remembered hearing about the time her grandmother said they ran from 'that Mexican' . . ." Much research followed before Cloud was able to piece together the story. She later noted, "It was not her grandmother [she meant], but her great-grandmother and the only grandmother living in Texas at the time."

9. Wayne Luther Capooth, *The History of the Millsaps* (Self-published: 1993].

10. Nettie Milsaps Gormanous, *The Milsaps Family, Patriotic, Hard Working, God Loving Americans* (Self-published: 1990), 12. Gormanous is a great-great-granddaughter of Isaac Millsaps.

11. Petition by Mary Millsaps, 9 May 1838, Texas State Archives, file No. 14.

12. Gormanous, *The Milsaps Family,* 13.

13. *Ibid.,* 15.

14. Henry Cardenas, telephone interview with author, San Antonio, Texas, 18 July 1995. Cardenas is a great-grandson of the Mexican *soldado* who carried the same last name. The *soldado*'s first name is unknown to Cardenas, who heard stories about his great-grandfather from his father, Enrique Trevino Cardenas.

15. Thomas B. Floyd to Esther Clark, 15 June 1855, typescript in personal file of Judy Deal.

16. Catherine Clark Griffin, Esther Clark's daughter, wrote the story of the Gonzales women at the house of Mrs. Braches, date unknown.

17. *Ibid.*

18. Tommie Stulting, "A Pioneer Woman And Her Family," 9. 1989. Stulting is a great-great-great-granddaughter of Esther Berry House Floyd Clark.

19. Catherine Clark Griffin, writings.

20. Robert Hancock Hunter, *The Narrative of Robert Hancock Hunter* (Austin: Encino Press), 21-24.

21. Unfortuntaley for Floyd descendants, no one knows if Esther ever wrote back to Dolphin's brother.

22. Ramon Vasquez y Sanchez, telephone interview with author, San Antonio, Texas, 15 January 1997. Sanchez is a great-great-grandson of a Mexican *soldado* whose name was believed to be Francisco Vasquez (or Basquez). He married Marcela Vasquez, who according to Sanchez, died in 1922 at the age of "either 105 or 106." Sanchez heard the story as a youngster from his grandmother, Maria Ybarra.

23. Santiago Rabia was a member of the Tampico Regiment. See the Santiago Rabia Papers, DRT Library.

24. Thomas Lloyd Miller, *Bounty and Donation Land Grants of Texas 1835–1888* (Austin & London: University of Texas Press), 242. Although family legend says Santiago changed his name from Rabia to Ravia when he pledged his allegiance to Texas, the switch probably occurred sometime after he received his land. The land grant states 640 acres were given to "Santiago Rabia."

25. Roger McMullen, telephone interview with author, Breckenridge, Texas, 17 July 1995. McMullen is a great-grandson of Santiago Rabia (Ravia).

26. Elizabeth Tumlinson Ashworth and Bobbie Rogers Thompson, letter

to author, 10 June 1995. Both descend from John Tumlinson, a brother to George Washington Tumlinson's father, James, Jr.

The story of James Tumlinson, Jr.'s trip to Bexar was told to Thompson by Rebecca Tumlinson, who heard the stories about her Alamo ancestor from her grandfather.

27. Helena Benavides Townsend, telephone interview with author, Brownsville, Texas, 17 May 1995. Townsend is a great-granddaughter of Rafael Morales. She grew up hearing stories of Morales from her grandmother, Maria de Jesus Morales, in downtown Brownsville.

28. Frances "Menefee" Sutherland to sister, "We Cousins" (Virginia to Texas), Volume I, which was compiled by Florence Sutherland Hudson of San Benito, Texas. Hudson copyrighted her work in 1957.

29. Gen. Sam Houston to Mary B. Lewis, 24 July 1836. Copy in the William Irvine Lewis file at the DRT Library.

30. "Reminiscences of the Alamo," *The Telegraph and Texas Register,* 21 October 1840.

31. *Ibid.*

32. Essie Walton Martin, "Some Scurlock History," *Texas State Genealogical Society Quarterly,* volume 33, number 2 (June 1993).

33. Essie Walton Martin, *The Scurlocks: Seekers of Freedom* (Self-published: 1985), 24-27.

34. *Ibid.,* 30-31. The story of Captain Scurlock's escape was told by a Judge Goodrich of Hemphill, Texas, to W. S. Horne of Houston. Horne was a grandson of Captain Scurlock and was at his home in 1885 when he died.

35. Captain William Scurlock's reunion with Ned Ragsdale was told to O. A. Seale in a 1927 letter from a Ragsdale descendant in Temple, Texas. Seale was a granddaughter of Captain Scurlock.

Index

About the Author

RON JACKSON is currently a reporter for *The Daily Oklahoman* in Oklahoma City. He began his journalism career in 1985, and worked ten and a half years for *The Reporter* in his hometown of Vacaville, California. He now makes his home in Rocky, Oklahoma, with his wife, Jeannia, and their two children, Joseph and Ashley. Jackson is a member of the Alamo Battlefield Association.